GOD'S WAY TO SUCCESS

Purpose & Goal Setting Journal

JENNIFER LEE SMITH

Teach us to number our days and recognize how few they are; help us to spend them as we should.- Psalm 90:12

CHAPTER 1

GOD SETS THE STANDARD FOR SUCCESS

God sets the standard for success

Success. What is it and why are we all so obsessed with it? In the church, outside of the church, we all seem to have this deep desire to succeed at something.

I find it fascinating that every video I've watched, book I've read or workshop I've attended on success, the experts, business coaches or success gurus ALWAYS include biblical principles in their strategy. It's fascinating because many of these people are unbelievers and have never even read the bible. They don't even know the principals they are teaching are found in the bible. Of course, that shouldn't surprise us as God is the Author of life and we could say the Bible is:

Basic
Instructions
Before
Leaving
Earth

In Genesis chapter 1 as God was creating, the Word says seven times *"He saw it was good"*. It gave Him satisfaction to create a beautiful, perfect, harmonious, fruitful world. It brought Him even greater satisfaction when He created man. In that verse He called it "very good". We are created in God's image; created to create, to be productive, to be fruitful, to bring praise and glory to God, to bless others and to find satisfaction in that. God wants us to be successful at what He calls us to do.

We see in the Garden of Eden (before the curse) that Adam was given work, work that was enjoyable and fulfilling. Work was never intended to be horrible. It was instilled in us to be about God's business. In Adam's case he was to tend and keep the land and name all the animals.

And yet, maybe you are thinking to yourself that your work is horrible. The environment, the boss or maybe the work is not something you enjoy. Please know this does not mean that you are out of God's will. We are now living in a fallen world. But God promises to use all things together for good for His children. So, take heart and know it's working out a greater purpose and if you are still in that job, it's a season and this season will pass. Be faithful right where you are. My prayer is that God's Way to Success will be used mightily by God to help you dream again and prepare you for what God is preparing for you!

"In route to your sweet spot make your current spot sweet."
David Benham

What is success?

The worlds view of success is usually power and prestige, fame and fortune. And if you buy into that it's shocking and confusing to hear about "successful" people committing suicide, overdosing, going into rehab, getting divorced, etc. Clearly, that is not success.

Even the wisest man who ever lived, King Solomon tried it the world's way and documents the futility and emptiness of doing so in Ecclesiastes. He had riches, fame, many wives and concubines, everything his heart desired and called it futility. If those things can't satisfy, then what can?

His conclusion, *"Even so, I have noticed one thing, at least, that is good. It is good for people to eat, drink, and enjoy their work under the sun during the short life God has given them, and to accept their lot in life. And it is a good thing to receive wealth from God and the good health to enjoy it. To enjoy your work and accept your lot in life—this is indeed a gift from God."* Ecclesiastes 5:18-20

And Ecclesiastes 12:13, *"Respect and obey God! This is what life is all about."*

"Our greatest fear should not be of failure, but of succeeding at something that doesn't really matter." Dwight L. Moody

"When God calls you to something, He is not always calling you to succeed, He's calling you to obey! The success of the calling is up to Him; the obedience is up to you." -David Wilkerson

It's important for you to define what success it looks like in your own life. Even before I completely accomplish my goals I define success as:

- To trust and love my God in all of life's circumstances
- To be faithful and do what God is calling me to do in all my roles
- To use my time, talents and resources to glorify God and bless others

Of course, as I set goals and make plans I do have a desired outcome. It is rewarding to successfully accomplish that which God has given you to do and when it comes to employment, well if you don't achieve the goals of the job, you'll soon be looking for a new one!

When I was in sales, the accomplishment of my monthly, quarterly and annual goals resulted in awards, monetary bonuses and intrinsic satisfaction for a job well done. My clients were blessed by the benefits of their purchase, I blessed my employer by bringing in clients and revenue and my employer blessed me. All of that glorifies God who loves us and loves to bless and see His creation enjoying good things.

Whether writing a book, raising great kids, paying cash for a brand new car, loving our spouses well, losing weight, eating healthy, getting clean off of drugs, adding 10 new clients, getting out of debt, making more than enough money to be generous, serving in a ministry, designing a space or cleaning the house, *whatever our hands finds to do (Ecclesiastes 9:10)* we should *do it heartily (with gusto) as unto the Lord (Colossians 3:23)* and when we have accomplished it, we should stand back, savor the moment, be proud and rejoice, enjoy the fruits of our labor and give thanks. It is good. Our Heavenly Father is proud of us.

"Blessings on all who reverence and trust the Lord—on all who obey him! Their reward shall be prosperity and happiness." Psalm 128:1-2

God designed you for a specific purpose, with a unique sphere of influence, experiences, and gifts and talents that will bless others, glorify Him and bring you closer in your walk with Jesus while you enjoy great fulfillment. When He created you in your mother's womb, he already set you apart and knew what He appointed you to do (Jeremiah 1:5). He also knew all the sins you would commit, all the sins that would be committed against you, all your mess, mistakes, drama and trauma your life would be and how He was going to weave that into a beautiful, one of a kind masterpiece. Oh, how glorious our God is!

"For we are God's masterpiece. He has created us anew in Christ Jesus, so we can do the good things he planned for us long ago." Ephesians 2:10

It doesn't matter if the dream or goal you have has already been done by thousands of people. You will reach people no one else can, in a way no one else can. What you bring to the table in all you do is unique and beautiful just the way God created it to be.

You can be assured the desire in you to succeed at what you put your hand to is from God. He is not a God of mediocrity. He is not a God of scarcity. He is not a God of fear. He is not a God of confusion or chaos.

He is God, our Father. Maker of heaven and earth. Lover of your soul. The God of endless mercy and grace. He is the God of excellence. He is the God of abundance. He is the God of power and love. He is the God of order and perfection. If you have put your trust in Jesus Christ and His finished work for you on the cross, this God is in you, empowering you and leading you. And if you've not yet believed on Him, putting your trust in Him to take away all your sin and be in relationship with you, know that He is pursuing you!

"And may the Lord our God show us his approval and make our efforts successful. Yes, make our efforts successful!" Psalm 90:17

Trials & Tribulations

I trust that we have all lived long enough in this world and we know our bibles well enough to know that even as favored, beloved children of God who Jesus came to give life more abundantly to, we will have trials and tribulations and we do live in a fallen world with a real enemy. We're not home yet.

This is no reason to not live with hopeful expectancy and set goals and dream big! Life is full of ups and downs and challenges and you could get very disillusioned when troubles come your way if you don't keep your eyes on the bigger picture and plans of our sovereign God.

With that being said, let's take a look at a different example of "success" from the bible.

Job- *"There once was a man named Job who lived in the land of Uz. He was blameless--a man of complete integrity. He feared God and stayed away from evil." Job 1:1*

Blameless. Integrity. Feared God. Stayed away from evil. A righteous man. He also had great wealth and a family whom he loved very much. Quite a success by anyone's standards.

But in a New York minute, everything can change. Unbeknownst to him behind the scenes God and Satan were talking about him. Satan accused Job of loving and reverencing God only because of all God had blessed him with. He was betting Job would turn on God if he lost everything. In this stunning behind the scenes look into the spiritual realm, God gave permission for Job to be tested. Job's children were killed, Job's wealth lost and then his health attacked.

"Then Job arose and tore his robe and shaved his head and fell on the ground and worshiped. And he said, "Naked I came from my mother's womb, and naked shall I return. The LORD gave, and the LORD has taken away; blessed be the name of the LORD." In all this Job did not sin or charge God with wrong." Job 1:20-22

It got worse. Job's friends went from welcome companions to accusing him of doing something to bring all this on. They never even bring up Satan and that this could be some kind of spiritual attack. They automatically assume the Job is being punished for some sin. But God in His perfect timing shows up, rebukes the accusations and restores Job double all he lost *after* He had Job pray for his accusing friends.

When was Job successful? Only at the beginning when he had it all? At the end when he had restoration? Yes, and yes! But I think you'd agree the most successful part of the story is his faithfulness and trust in the midst of the attack. Instead of turning on God, *"he worshiped"*! *"He did not sin or charge God with wrong."* Wow.

Here we are thousands of years later being encouraged and inspired by the book of Job. Countless people have understanding of the unseen world and been emboldened in their faith and confidence in God's sovereignty because of Job. I'd call that success.

"And without faith it is impossible to please God, because anyone who comes to him must believe that he exists and that he rewards those who earnestly seek him." Hebrews 11:6

Joseph- Joseph went from being the favorite son, loved and doted on by his father, to being thrown into a pit by his jealous brothers, sold into slavery, accused of a crime he didn't commit, and forgotten about in prison.

God had given him a literal dream of being in authority. This was a destiny Joseph could not have planned or prepared for himself.

It takes strong maturity, great faith and dependence on the Lord to be a great leader. One must love and trust to obey God in hard things. That was exactly the training Joseph would need for his calling. In the midst of what certainly would not have been part of Joseph's goals for his life, we see that even as a slave he had success.

*"The LORD was with Joseph, and he became a **successful** man, and he was in the house of his Egyptian master. His master saw that the LORD was with him and that the LORD caused all that he did to **succeed** in his hands. So Joseph found favor in his sight and attended him, and he made him overseer of his house and put him in charge of all that he had."*
Genesis 37:2-5

In the end Joseph becomes second in authority in Egypt, has saved the land from a famine, has family of his own and is reconciled to his brothers and dad. He is a success in all these ways and in his attitude and trust of God's sovereignty saying to his brother's, *"As for you, you meant evil against me, but God meant it for good, to bring it about that many people should be kept alive, as they are today." Genesis 50:20*

Anguish and heartbreak are made sweet by the success that comes out of it. One of the biggest pieces of that is gaining God's perspective in a situation.

I've seen it in my own life. My dad's unexpected death that drew me to my knees, sweetly broken at the foot of the cross. The grace of God in that situation that led me, a drug addict out of an addiction and healed the wounds that held me there. How He has brought that full circle to a ministry serving Him and loving others who are in bondage. What a bittersweet success.

"And we know that all things work together for good to them that love God, to them who are the called according to his purpose." Romans 8:28

Christian, the calling on your life is bigger than you have imagined. His grace and power are bigger than you have imagined. Nothing you do in obedience to Him goes unnoticed or unrewarded. The bigger the calling, the bigger your faith and your maturity in Christ have to be.

- "Consider it pure joy, my brothers and sisters, whenever you face trials of many kinds, because you know that the testing of your faith produces perseverance. Let perseverance finish its work so that you may be mature and complete, not lacking anything." James 1:2-4
- "Wickedness never brings real success; only the godly have that." Proverbs 12:3

- "My success—at which so many stand amazed—is because you are my mighty protector." Psalm 71:7

- "Be strong and very courageous. Be careful to obey all the law my servant Moses gave you; do not turn from it to the right or to the left, that you may be successful wherever you go. Keep this Book of the Law always on your lips; meditate on it day and night, so that you may be careful to do everything written in it. **Then you will be prosperous and successful.** Joshua 1:7-8

What's it All About?

It's not about following our career path;
It's about following His call upon our lives. Matthew 16:24

It's not about our self-efforts to live for Him;
It's about letting Him live His life in us. Galatians 2:20

It's not about our attempts at self-improvement;
It's about His transforming grace. 2 Corinthians 5:17

It's not about our self-image;
It's about being conformed to His image. Romans 8:29

It's not about our abilities to serve;
It's about His power to equip us. Acts 1:8

It's not about our human resources;
It's about His sufficiency. 2 Corinthians 3:5

It's not about wanting the approval of others;
It's about having His approval. 2 Timothy 2:15

CHAPTER 2

GOD KNOWS THE PLAN

God knows the plan

Joseph didn't expect the evils that were committed against him. He didn't plan that someone's sin or even his own sin or naïve mistakes would work together to accomplish God's plan. But that is the great God we serve using everything together for our good and His glory.

As you make your plans, you must remain flexible as God directs your paths. We cannot put God in a box. We cannot begin to imagine the things God has in store for us.

Think back 10 years ago. Did you imagine you'd be where you are now, dealing with the challenges you are now? The blessings you have? The daily interactions you have? Maybe generally you can but the specifics are hard to predict. We really don't know. And while there are definitely seasons where big changes occur, many times life happens slowly and subtly as the path veers.

We see Joseph's secret to success was simply to be obedient in each decision. As Jesus said in Matthew 6:33, "But seek first the kingdom of God and His righteousness, and all these things will be added to you." He couldn't break out of prison and go knock on the palace door and announce he was ready to be second in command. First of all, he had no idea that was the plan and secondly even if he knew that was the plan, that would not have worked! Instead unbeknownst to him, God was opening the doors. As Joseph obeyed, he walked through each door one day at a time, one step at a time right into those palace doors.

"Trust God and do the next thing." -Oswald Chambers

"You will keep him in perfect peace, whose mind is stayed on You, Because he trusts in You." Isaiah 26:3

Does that mean we shouldn't make our plans? Does this mean we do nothing and just wait for God to open doors? No. Not at all. I just want you to be aware God's plans are so big we can't fathom them! And you may be in a season where you feel stifled and discouraged by small steps. Don't be. Dream big! Make your plans! God has an eraser where He wants bigger plans. He also guides you and gives you desires, ideas and plans so write 'em down!

"...Write the vision; make it plain on tablets, so he may run who reads it." Habakkuk 2:2

"Do not despise these small beginnings, for the LORD rejoices to see the work begin, to see the plumb line in Zerubbabel's hand." Zechariah 4:10

The ultimate goal

The greatest adventure we can go on in this life is to know Christ. With Christ as the center of your world everything you do flows from that. He is involved in every detail and with every step of every goal that He puts in your mind and heart, you will know Him better and better and see His hand at work in and through you. Knowing Christ is the ultimate goal.

"I want to know Christ—yes, to know the power of his resurrection and participation in his sufferings, becoming like him in his death, and so, somehow, attaining to the resurrection from the dead. Not that I have already obtained all this, or have already arrived at my goal, but I press on to take hold of that for which Christ Jesus took hold of me. Brothers and sisters, I do not consider myself yet to have taken hold of it. But one thing I do: Forgetting what is behind and straining toward what is ahead, I press on toward the goal to win the prize for which God has called me heavenward in Christ Jesus." Philippians 3:10-14

Do this with God

What you have in your hands is part journal, part goal setting workbook and part daily planner. Every bit of it however, is designed for you to do with The Wonderful Counselor, our Teacher, Comforter, the One who knows the plan He has for you. Invite Him into this. Pray as you read and journal and believe He desires to answer you and encourage you more than you desire to receive it.

"Now listen, you who say, "Today or tomorrow we will go to this or that city, spend a year there, carry on business and make money." Why, you do not even know what will happen tomorrow. What is your life? You are a mist that appears for a little while and then vanishes. Instead, you ought to say, "If it is the Lord's will, we will live and do this or that." James 4:13-15

Think of this book like a roadmap for your year. The route is open to change but you've at least got to have some idea of where you are going. When you know where you are going, you will be more intentional and make steady progress and steps in the right direction under the guidance and dependence on God.

God wants you to trust His good plan.

Do you find it hard to believe that God has amazing plans for you? Maybe you think you've blown it? Maybe you think that you can't hear Him so how could you possibly get onboard? Truth bomb! All of those thoughts are lies!

Read over and mediate (ponder) the truth and promises in these verses on plans:

- "Commit to the Lord whatever you do,
  and he will establish your plans." Proverbs 16:3

- Delight yourself in the LORD, and he will give you the desires of your heart. Psalm 37:4

- "For I know the plans I have for you, declares the Lord, plans to prosper you and not to harm you, plans to give you hope and a future." Jeremiah 29:11

- "May he give you the desire of your heart
  and make all your plans succeed." Psalm 20:4

- "In their hearts humans plan their course,
  but the Lord establishes their steps." Proverbs 16:9

- "Let the morning bring me word of your unfailing love,
  for I have put my trust in you. Show me the way I should go, for to you I entrust my life." Psalm 143:8

- "Many are the plans in a person's heart, but it is the Lord's purpose that prevails." Proverbs 19:21

- "All this also comes from the Lord Almighty, whose plan is wonderful, whose wisdom is magnificent." Isaiah 28:29

Let's look at 2 of these verses that have conditional promises, meaning if you do something then God does something.

"Commit to the Lord whatever you do,
and he will establish your plans." Proverbs 16:3

What does it mean to commit? (Use a dictionary)

_____

_____

_____

_____

What are some ways you can commit your work to the Lord?

_____

_____

_____

_____

"Delight yourself in the LORD, and he will give you the desires of your heart." Psalm 37:4

What does it mean to delight? (Use a dictionary)

_____

_____

_____

_____

What are some ways you can delight in the Lord?

_____

_____

_____

_____

CHAPTER 3

Limiting Beliefs
&
Fears of
Inadequacies

Limiting Beliefs & Fears of Inadequacies

I've discovered something profound in myself since I became self-employed and in the Christian women I've coached in my success planning and goal setting workshops; most of the previous year's goals not accomplished **were not** due to external circumstances but rather internal beliefs from lies they believed, limiting beliefs and fears of inadequacy.

These are often times strongholds that need to be torn down.

Here is the list of the most frequently heard "reasons" I've heard for women not accomplishing their goals:

1. Feeling like a fraud, inadequate, unqualified
2. Comparison
3. Afraid to go out of comfort zone
4. People pleasing, Lack of boundaries
5. Procrastination & Perfectionism
6. Negative Emotions
7. Wrong Beliefs about God

"For though we walk in the flesh, we do not war according to the flesh. For the weapons of our warfare are not carnal but mighty in God for pulling down strongholds, casting down arguments and every high thing that exalts itself against the knowledge of God, bringing every thought into captivity to the obedience of Christ..." 2 Corinthians 10:3-5

I broached this subject gently but now I want to call these reasons what they really are, excuses. Yes, you heard me right. It's not that I am not empathic or that I have not (or do not) struggle with these feelings, but let me define excuse and then maybe you'll agree with me.

Billy Sunday said, *"An excuse is the skin of a reason stuffed with a lie."*

It sounds reasonable but in actuality it is a lie. We may believe it but never the less it is a lie that threatens to keep us from taking action on the desires and plans God has put in us. Who stands to gain from that? You guessed it, Satan. Jesus tells us Satan's mission statement and also what He came to do in John 10:10, *"The thief does not come except to steal, and to kill, and to destroy. I have come that they may have life, and that they may have it more abundantly."*

Indeed, our flesh cooperates with the lies of Satan and we can find ourselves with a stronghold and no closer to our goals then we were when we started. Scripture tells us to be aware of Satan's schemes, *"in order that Satan might not outwit us."* 2 Corinthians 2:11

In this section I want to address some of these strongholds that I've struggled with as a middle-aged woman starting a new career and the solutions I've found in God's Word. If you share any of these, I pray you'll recognize them and walk in the victory Jesus already gave you so you can be successful with the goals God has given you. If you do not relate to these examples I hope that you will be able to apply the overall message of this chapter; to do what God is calling you to do regardless of the feeling of fear. Just do it afraid!

Jesus loves you with a perfect love. You have nothing to fear.

"There is no fear in love, but perfect love casts out fear. For fear has to do with punishment, and whoever fears has not been perfected in love." 1 John 4:18

"I feel like a fraud, I feel unqualified"

You know who also felt unqualified for the calling God had on his life? Gideon. Listen to his assignment and his response.

*So Israel was reduced to starvation by the Midianites. Then the Israelites cried out to the LORD for help...Gideon son of Joash was threshing wheat at the bottom of a winepress to hide the grain from the Midianites. The angel of the LORD appeared to him and said, **"Mighty hero**, the LORD is with you!"*

Then the LORD turned to him and said, "Go with the strength you have, and rescue Israel from the Midianites. I am sending you!"

"But Lord," Gideon replied, "how can I rescue Israel? My clan is the weakest in the whole tribe of Manasseh, and I am the least in my entire family!"

The LORD said to him, "I will be with you. And you will destroy the Midianites as if you were fighting against one man." Judges 6:12-16

Let's just break that down:

- There is a famine going on and the people cry out to the Lord.
- The Lord hears their prayers and chooses Gideon to rescue the Israelites.
- The Lord lets Gideon know his assignment and addresses him as "Mighty Hero".
- The Lord instructs Gideon to," *Go with the strength you have...*"
- Gideon immediately replies that his clan is the weakest and he is the least.
- The Lord reframes it for Gideon letting him know that He will be with Him. He doesn't even address Gideon's doubts about weakness or him being the least.

God doesn't make mistakes. He saw Gideon as a mighty hero. He didn't ask Gideon to do it in his own strength, he wanted Gideon to go in the strength he did have but the empowerment and victory was going to come from the Lord being with Him. The Lord clearly states He will be with him and that Gideon would easily destroy the Midianites. Simply stated, Gideon is a chosen vessel for the Lord.

Have you ever felt inadequate or unqualified or like God is making a mistake sending you? Or maybe you have felt like you just don't belong in a certain circle, an occupation, or a group of people. Like they have made a mistake and sooner or later they will discover who you really are and reject you?

I have. From a public speaking mishap to embarking on a new career in my forties, there have been plenty of times I've felt like an imposter even while I knew I was in God's perfect will for my life. Deep down I always believed God called me to write, teach and speak. Even as a child I knew it and always wanted to be on stage.

At my previous job working for a business publication part of my job was to represent the company to the business community. That meant a lot of big events that we sponsored. I was asked to address a crowd of 500 people with a few words to acknowledge the organization. It was only a few sentences that I had to say. As I looked around the room I saw so many "important" people that I felt inadequate to be on the stage like some VIP. Even though I was very successful at my job my thoughts were **"I feel like a fraud, I feel unqualified".** When I got up there every public speaking fear came to life and as I began to speak I forgot to breathe! And rather than take a breath and continue, I said as much as I could in that one breath and had to stop. I felt like such an imposter so without even finishing, I simply left the stage! I cannot express to you how awful the rest of that breakfast was.

I was not walking in the Spirit, realizing the fact that God had sent me and that He was with me. All I had to do was show up and obey Him. It was His favor and His strength that would empower me. I was in the flesh worrying about what others would think of me. Fear of man truly is a snare.

The world has something they call Imposter Syndrome. Wikipedia describes imposter syndrome like this, "*high-achieving individuals marked by an inability to internalize their accomplishments and a persistent fear of being exposed as a "fraud". Despite external evidence of their competence, those exhibiting the syndrome remain convinced that they are frauds and do not deserve the success they have achieved. Proof of success is dismissed as luck, timing, or as a result of deceiving others into thinking they are more intelligent and competent than they believe themselves to be. Some studies suggest that impostor syndrome is particularly common among high-achieving women. "*

We could say it is a result of us not believing our identity in Christ, His power and His calling on our lives.

"You live up to your identity not your potential." Jim Forton

The flesh was so concerned with what they would think of me that I wasn't thinking about who I am in Christ or that God had assigned this to me, or the fact that in all I do should be done *as unto the Lord*. In obedience, I should have represented my employer to the best of my ability. I should have blessed those in the audience with my words. I should have glorified God. That is where my thoughts should have been. I should have taken my thoughts captive to the obedience of Jesus Christ and not allowed those defeating statements, the lies, and the limiting beliefs to trip me up.

Thankfully that incident would not be allowed by our Great God to stop His plan for me.

A couple of years later after I left that job, the Lord gave me the opportunity to speak to a group of 150 business women at a luncheon where I would be the main speaker and speak for 25 minutes sharing my testimony of how the Lord had delivered me from an addiction to methamphetamines.

I had been sharing my testimony for years with small groups and individuals but now I'd be sharing it with business people, people that were our ideal client for our painting and color consulting company.

Did I really want total strangers to possibly think less of me? What if they judged me? What if I lost a potential client? **"I am afraid to be vulnerable. I am afraid of the critics."** But I knew God was calling me to do it, I knew it was for His glory and that He would use it to encourage others, so instead of it being about me, instead of allowing that voice to call me an imposter- causing me to focus on myself and walk in the flesh, I kept my eyes on glorifying God, bragging about Him.

That day **God** got a standing ovation from my words and our business has not suffered in the least, but rather it connected me to those women in a way that otherwise may not have happened. I had women that I would have never expected come up afterwards and thank me for giving them hope for their loved ones (and I'm sure for some of them personally).

Since then I have released a book and a biblical coaching package **The Way Out**, for overcoming drugs and alcohol. Talk about going public! On Facebook and YouTube, I share the stuff that is dark and shameful, yet that's how God is using me to reach women that won't come to church or ask for help.

God is hearing their silent cries for deliverance. Like Gideon's story these people are crying out for deliverance. Will I obey God and let Him use me?

Are there critics? Oh yes, I am sure there are. I have no doubt that unbelievers and people looking to criticize me watch those videos and may think I am an imposter, a fraud, not qualified to help others since I do not have a PhD. If I were to focus on them I would not accomplish what God calls me to do. So I pray for a tough skin and a tender heart. And I watch God open doors I never expected.

In what ways (if any) are you struggling with feeling like a fraud or being afraid to be vulnerable?

_____

_____

_____

_____

How can we conquer imposter syndrome?

- *1 Corinthians 3:5 says "It is not that we think we are qualified to do anything on our own. Our qualification comes from God."*
- *2 Corinthians 5:7 Walk by faith and not by sight (or feelings)*
- *Ask God to confirm the work of our hands- Psalm 90:17*

The takeaway: God has given us our gifts, talents, desires and will bring opportunities so focus on glorifying Him and blessing others.

"I'm not as talented as…" "Why is God blessing her and not me?"

Comparison is another trap that Satan likes to set. I said it earlier but I will say it again, you are unique. No one else has your sphere of influence, your experience, your expertise, your talents, skills, gifts and personality. God really does have a custom fit mission for you.

I have seen in my walk as a Christian that God moves people in the body many times in the same direction which makes a lot of sense since there is a lot of work to be done and He needs all hands-on deck so to speak. We shouldn't be surprised when He calls us to a similar mission as someone else. The need is too great for just one of us to fill.

Once I started writing this book and shared it with others, I had a friend say God had put it in her heart to write and speak about the same thing. She should because she is going to reach people that I won't. Even if we have some of the same people that we know, one of us will resonate more with the listener, or we will both confirm the same thing. If we view it in the Spirit and through the lens of God, there is no competition and no comparison.

In our flesh we can be unhealthy in competition and in our comparisons. I do not believe that competition itself is ungodly. It's only when it holds you back from obeying God or creates unrighteous anger or any other ungodly attitude that it is a problem.

We see after Jesus rose from the dead (but hadn't yet ascended) that He tells Peter the manner in which Peter will die. Then we see Peter look at John the apostle and say to Jesus, *"What about him, Lord?"* Jesus replied, *"If I want him to remain alive until I return, what is that to you? As for you, follow me."* John 21:21

It's really important to Jesus that we keep our eyes on Him and follow Him not worrying about what He is doing with someone else. *"...let us run with endurance the race that is set before us, looking to Jesus, the founder and perfecter of our faith..." Hebrews 12:1-2*

"I don't want to go out of my comfort zone"

It's easy to be complacent. You don't even see the outcome of it until something wakes you up to it. Relationships, careers, health, all can be stagnant and remain healthy for a time but it won't be long until you find yourself in an unhealthy situation and settling for mediocrity. Going out of your comfort zone is the way to conquer complacency and the only way you will accomplish goals that are worth accomplishing.

When I quit a good job to work for my husband, and then started my own business it was exciting. I felt alive and hopeful for the future. Yet, it involved going out of my comfort zone.

- ✓ Having to learn new things with no guaranteed paycheck was definitely outside my comfort zone.

- ✓ Sharing my testimony of past drug addiction (with people who may not understand and may judge me) was outside of my comfort zone.

- ✓ Doing Facebook livestreams and being vulnerable to grow my ministry and my business are outside of my comfort zone.

- ✓ Learning from my mistakes although very effective, is also outside of my comfort zone.

I am learning to embrace the growth that comes and the dependence it creates for me to lean hard into Jesus in order to be fully alive and pursuing God and His calling for me. And it turns out it gets easier as you practice it. Really what is the alternative? Living in mediocrity? May it never be so!

"Behold the turtle. He makes progress only when he sticks his neck out."- James Bryant Conant

In the first chapter of Joshua, God tells Joshua three times to be "strong and courageous" as they enter the promised land. He assures Joshua, *"I will give you every place where you set your foot, as I promised Moses."*

Forty years earlier though, Joshua and Caleb (another man of faith) had been part of 12 spies sent to spy out the land. When they returned excited about the land "flowing with milk and honey", the other 10 were afraid to go out of their comfort zones *even though God had promised them the land!* Even with encouragement and admonition from Joshua and Caleb- *"Do not rebel against the LORD, and don't be afraid of the people of the land. They are only helpless prey to us! They have no protection, but the LORD is with us! Don't be afraid of them!" Numbers 13:9*- the people still refused.

Instead the people rebelled against God and protested saying, *"If only we had died in Egypt, or even here in the wilderness!"* they complained. *"Why is the LORD taking us to this country only to have us die in battle? Our wives and our little ones will be carried off as plunder! Wouldn't it be better for us to return to Egypt?" Numbers 14:2-3*

Wow! These were the same people who saw God part the Red Sea as He delivered them from slavery in Egypt, yet they wouldn't believe that God would be with them, provide for them, protect them and bless them. Here is God's response to their lack of belief, *"And the LORD said to Moses, "How long will these people treat me with contempt? Will they never believe me, even after all the miraculous signs I have done among them?"*

If only they had gone outside of their comfort zones and believed God's promises they would not have wandered in the wilderness for forty years.

We are the children of God. We have a personal relationship and He is our Daddy. He is the perfect parent and can be trusted. Your faith is pleasing to Him. Don't live with the "if only"!

What promises had God given you about "taking the land"? What ways are you struggling with going outside of your comfort zone?

Finding the right people to work with

Do you remember the story of Peter when He stepped out of the boat and walked on water? **As long as He kept His eyes on Jesus he was able to do it.** As soon as the waves came up and he took his eyes off Jesus he sank. Your waves are those circumstances that make you fear and want to be safe. What did Jesus say to Him as He pulled Peter out of the water? *"Oh ye of little faith, why didn't you believe?"*

How can we conquer complacency, go outside of our comfort zones and please God with our faith?

- Keep your eyes on Jesus, trust Him even if the circumstances scare you, or the fears of inadequacy come.
- Hold on to His promises.
- Look to God alone for validation and approval.
- Practice taking active steps of faith every day.

"Do one thing every day that scares you."
- Eleanor Roosevelt

Takeaway: Gods work is always a transformation from the inside out- so how you think will impact how you feel, and subsequently the actions you take.

Think on God's Word and His promises.

"This is my command—be strong and courageous! Do not be afraid or discouraged. For the Lord your God is with you wherever you go." Joshua 1:9

"God has not given us a spirit of fear but of power, love and a sound mind." 2 Timothy 1:7

"Without faith it is impossible to please Him..." Hebrews 11:6

"I want people to like me."

People pleasing is one of those areas where we can see how the devil masquerades as an angel of light. I mean aren't we called to love others? Shouldn't we put their needs before our own?

As I write this I can hear the slick, hissing sound of a deceiver taking God's word out of context in the Garden of Eden, in the wilderness with Christ and in our own lives as Satan tries to deceive us to do seemingly "good" or reasonable things that in the end are not God's perfect will.

As Holy Spirit filled believers we really do have a desire to love and serve others. But at what cost? Paul the apostle says in Galatians 1:10 "Am I now trying to win the approval of human beings, or of God? Or am I trying to please people? If I were still trying to please people, I would not be a servant of Christ."

Like Jesus, we need to be about our Fathers business, whatever that may look like for us individually. The one thing that will be consistent is doing what's right, not compromising our faith in order to please others and making disciples. We need to set boundaries.

"The fear of man brings a snare, but he who trusts in the LORD will be exalted." Proverbs 29:25

There are many compromises we can make as people pleasers that manifest differently, but the one I am most aware in this season of my life is on how I spend my time. I think that is because now that I work from home I've enjoyed my flexibility and being able to enjoy my friends a little more- enjoying 2 hours lunches and visits in the middle of the day. But that meant I would have to work in the evening and take away time from my husband and things we like to do. I began to realize that that was irresponsible on my part. My actions didn't line up with my real priorities.

When I worked for someone else I would have never treated their business this way, so why was I treating my business and my husband's business this way? I could no longer justify it. I realized I had a problem with people pleasing as I found myself struggling to say no or over explaining when I said no. I needed to set boundaries.

"So be careful how you live. Don't live like fools, but like those who are wise. Make the most of every opportunity in these evil days." Ephesians 5:15-16

Time is short. We need to make sure we are using it for the priorities God has given us. In this season of my life I am building a business and without a guaranteed paycheck it is imperative that I am making every effort to do that. Otherwise I will have to go back to work for someone else, which **is not** what I believe God is calling me to in this season.

I also make it a point to see or call my mom every day. Since 2013 she and I have been faithfully praying together every day. Once a month we get together for dinner. I lost my dad unexpectedly when he was 54. I lost my brother unexpectedly at 46. Needless to say, I am very aware that we are not promised tomorrow, and I need to cherish each moment I get with her.

Why would I allow people pleasing and lack of boundaries to take me away from what's truly important to God and me?

Maybe you are building a business, going for a promotion at work, serving in a ministry or going back to school. Maybe you are trying to repair a shaky marriage or you have little ones at home. Whatever season you are in- figure out your priorities and build your life and boundaries accordingly. People will understand. And if they don't- it's not on you to convince them.

"Teach us to number our days and recognize how few they are; help us to spend them as we should." Psalm 90:12

The other way God has been showing me that I can be a people pleaser is not wanting to offend others or speak up in certain situations.

One of the things Jesus delivered me from was New Age/Occult. However, I still have many friends and continue to make friends that are deep into New Age philosophies. They do not know what the bible says about such practices so quite innocently they have invited me to participate in things they believe to be good but I know the bible warns against. It would be easier to make an excuse about being busy, not be friends anymore or to go along with what they are doing. But those ways would not be pleasing to God or beneficial to others.

Instead of running away from these friendships, I prayerfully speak the truth in love to the best of my ability, gently and without quarrels in the way I believe Jesus would answer them. I'm not perfect in these situations, but I am obedient. In one such case one my friends actually thanked me for being honest and although she believes differently than I do, went out of her way to hear my opinion. She and I are grateful that we could have a friendship despite our beliefs and that I didn't take the easy way out and retreat from the conversation.

In another case I did compromise my beliefs in an effort to not offend a client and went along with something that turned out to be very dangerous.

I was doing a strategic planning session with a client who would begin each session with an opening prayer- much like we as Christians would. I stood in the circle with them around an altar they had set up. They began speaking in their language so I didn't know exactly what they were praying but they then interpreted for those of us who did not speak their language. Turns out one of things they were doing was praying to what they called mother earth. To top it off they were praying (talking to and calling on) their ancestors and inviting then to come and guide them.

While they would not have called it a séance, that is essentially what it was. It was beyond a shadow of a doubt idolatry on my part. I was there with them. I was part of the circle. I was in essence in agreement with them as I stood in front of the altar while they straight up invited a spirit other than the Holy Spirit of God, and gave permission for it to come and guide. I entered into it not knowing what they were going to do but, in the end, stayed in the circle because I did not want to offend them!

When God addresses the Israelites in Hosea for their idolatry He says, *"My people are destroyed for lack of knowledge..." Hosea 4:6*

Of course, I should have known better. I was delivered from the occult and I know the dark power. I can only imagine how the enemy was full of glee to see me standing there giving him permission to come into my life!

I had a Believer try to reassure me afterwards who asked what I was doing and thinking as this was happening. Their point was that perhaps it wasn't as bad as I was making it out to be since I was praying in Jesus name in my head the whole time and since I of course confessed and repented immediately. My response to them was I totally get that and I receive God's grace and forgiveness and power over the enemy. However, there was still consequences for giving Satan an open door and for committing spiritual adultery. And adultery was indeed what it was. If what I was thinking in my head made what I was doing ok, then the same argument could be applied if I was committing adultery on my husband. It certainly wouldn't make it ok to commit adultery if while I was in the act I kept my eyes closed and thought only about my husband. That is still adultery!

The destruction that followed was swift and horrific. Within 2 days and all in less than 2 weeks, 3 of my cats died terrible, bizarre and unexpected deaths. It's pretty unbelievable and of course I can't prove that it was a result of what I did, but I believe it was. I saw a lot of crazy destructive stuff during my time in New Age while I was an ignorant follower of Christ that convinces me this was not some coincidence. When you involve yourself in any practice against God, *especially as a Believer who already has a target on their back in the spiritual realm*, you give Satan territory. God of course forgave me for what I'd done and I'm covered by the blood of Jesus Christ, but there were still some devastating supernatural consequences that came with it.

I can't stress it enough, there is a reason God forbids us to get involved in New Age or Pagan practices. God only wants to protect us so He warns us and tells us how strongly He feels about it. His children should have no part in it.

"You cannot drink the cup of the Lord and the cup of demons too; you cannot have a part in both the Lord's table and the table of demons." 1 Corinthians 10:21

"There shall not be found among you anyone who makes his son or his daughter pass through the fire, one who uses divination, one who practices witchcraft, or one who interprets omens, or a sorcerer, or one who casts a spell, or a medium, or a spiritist, or one who calls up the dead. For whoever does these things is detestable to the LORD; and because of these detestable things the LORD your God will drive them out before you." Deuteronomy 18:10-12

I did learn from that tragedy and the next time I was doing a strategic planning with clients who held the same beliefs, I spoke up gently and without accusation and simply stated that because of my spiritual beliefs I could not be a part of the circle. You know what? Everyone was fine with that. I simply stepped away from the circle, turned my back and prayed to God.

It is simply not worth the price you pay to be a people pleaser.

"Be who you are and say what you feel, because those who mind don't matter and those who matter don't mind."
- Bernard Baruch

In what ways are you struggling with people pleasing? Have you faced consequences for going against God or your better judgment and instead fearing and following people? What were those consequences?

_____
_____
_____
_____
_____
_____

...be as wise as serpents and yet as harmless as doves. Matthew 10:16

- **Learn to say no and not worry if people don't understand.** Don't be rude or obnoxious about it or try to avoid the situation and not return calls- *Proverbs 3:3-4 says "Don't ever forget kindness and truth. Wear them like a necklace. Write them on your heart as if on a tablet. Then you will be respected and will please both God and people."* It is possible to say no, be God centered and others centered while speaking the truth in love.

- **Know the enemy of best is good**. There are lots of good things you can do with your time that crowd out *the best thing*. Get alone with God and your schedule and the demands that people are putting on you. He will give you the direction, the wisdom and the power to do what pleases Him with your time and talents.

- **Let your yes be yes and your no be no. Set boundaries and keep them.**

- **Get over the thought that you may miss an opportunity if you say no**. Trust God's wisdom, favor and sovereignty in your life.

"I can't charge for that"

It was quite easy to make money for others. That was my job. I also had to pay my bills and be a responsible contributing member of society. That pleases God. Like any wise person I always tried to make the most money that I could whether it was in negotiations when offered a job or in sales working hard to make my goals. I didn't have any overanalyzing or wrong beliefs holding me back.

But working for myself revealed that I had a stronghold. Because the talents and skills I charge for come so easily to me I don't always see them as valuable.

For as long as I'd been clean from drugs and walking closely with the Lord I KNEW God had called me to vocational ministry. But after I, the prodigal daughter, returned to the Father, He led me to secular employment as He restored all that Satan had stolen from me (or all I'd willingly given over in my foolishness). I enjoyed the restoration of a house, a car, a comfortable life of paying my bills on time, being debt free, credit card free, being able to be generous with tithes and offerings, helping those in need, and paying all my back taxes from the 7 years I had neglected to file.

More than that though, I had a passion for those who have no desire to go to a church to hear about Jesus, so it made perfect sense that I'd be placed in businesses where I'd develop relationships and be able to share my testimony and how awesome Jesus is with those God sent me to. It turned out that wherever God placed me I really was in full-time vocational ministry.

For 10 years I worked for others and at the same time I volunteered for 10 years as the leader and teacher of the Women's Drug & Alcohol ministry at Calvary Church of Albuquerque. When God called me out to quit my job and instead help my husband's business doing his marketing and expanding our services by adding architectural color consulting and redesign I was thrilled.

I had no idea that God had other, additional plans for me. Wonderful plans. Plans that He had already placed desires in my heart for. It started with me rewriting the curriculum for the ministry, then me being invited to speak at Christian women's events, then writing another bible study with a friend and being a founding member of a non-profit Christian women's conference. What amazing opportunities and blessings to be doing things I knew I was called to and was being empowered by God to do well using my gifts, talents, skills and all my experiences.

Problem was those things were taking a lot of time away from my work and not making any money. I trust God and know He is my Provider yet the bills began to stack up. That left me with quite a dilemma. Clearly it was not God's will for us to get into debt and for my husband to feel all the pressure to supply for a two income family while I'm out helping other people. ***My first ministry had to be at home.***

I was confronted with a limiting belief I didn't realize I had. After doing ministry for free for so long I believed that freely I had been given, freely I should share. Which is scriptural yet the free part is not necessarily referring to money. I had unconsciously decided that to charge money for any of the ministry I was doing was greedy and wrong. *Interestingly, I didn't believe that for other people, just for me.*

As with all strongholds from Satan, limiting beliefs start with a lie and only the truth will set us free. Satan's whole mission is to steal, kill and destroy. The resulting consequence of that lie was I put a huge strain on our finances, a strain on my marriage and became sick with worry and overwhelmed with confusion. *How could I do what God called me to do and cause so much destruction?*

I had to charge for my time and my products and services.

If I didn't I would have had to go back to work for someone else fulltime which would mean I could no longer help others in the way I believed God wanted me to.

While we are talking about money let's also remember that money cannot buy happiness. I agree that it is a big stress reliever when you aren't trying to figure out how you'll pay your bills. But only God brings us true peace and joy. Money itself is neutral. There are many miserable people with lots of money. And lots of what we'd consider poor people with more joy and peace. Money is a tool for many things but it's not a guarantee for happiness.

*"For the **love of money** is a root of all kinds of evil. Some people, eager for money, have wandered from the faith and pierced themselves with many griefs." 1 Timothy 6:10-14*

This verse is clear it is the *love of money*, not money itself that is a root of all evil. As I began tearing down this stronghold of thinking, "I can't charge for this" here are some thoughts I had to ponder:

1. **When I worked for others, I was using gifts and talents that God had given me.** There was an expectation that I was to do the job to the best of my ability serving others and selling the most I could- at the highest amount possible to profit the company. If I didn't perform then I wouldn't have a job. Doing my job well was a win-win for me and the company. My extra compensation in bonuses was not greedy but well-deserved. I was not serving money but I was serving God by doing all things heartily as unto Him. In my own business and vocational ministry, I had to ask myself these questions:

   -Did I believe what I had to offer was valuable?
   -Would I have paid for a solution to my problems when I was in that place in my life?
   -What is the cost to me and the cost to others if I don't charge for my services?

2. **It was actually selfish and foolish to not charge for my time.** It is never God's will for us to be in debt and be a slave. That hinders our ability to be free and generous in our families and for the kingdom of God. It causes unnecessary stress on your health, your marriage and family. I realize there are times in life that financial problems may happen- no fault of our own- and God can and will use them to show us our dependence on Him. But as an able-bodied woman in my prime of life living in America- with no children and a great work ethic- my husband should not be under so much pressure to take care of everything while I serve everyone else for free.

3. **When Jesus sent out His disciples to do the work of the Kingdom, He told them a worker was worthy of their wages.** I didn't have a problem with my pastor making a living from the church and the books he's written. In fact I supported that. I mean could he be half as amazing as he was in his calling if he was working a fulltime job

at a hospital? What about all the other people who worked at the church? Or the resources like videos and radio shows and websites and all the ways I had been reached and transformed by God through technology. What if these people thought they were being greedy or that it wasn't right to charge others and ended up saying no to God's call on their lives and going back to a job they weren't called to? I began to see the lie and the strategy behind this accusation from Satan.

4. **In all things it is God's will for me to be holy and to be dependent on Him**. If I had not gone through the financial struggle and the challenges I may not have leaned so strongly on Him. I may not have sought His perfect will for me if I didn't have to continually question it. I may not have built my faith by holding on to His promises. I may not have looked different from the world. Because of the new nature He has given me, I do desire to be holy and in His perfect will and He is the only Sovereign One, not me.

How could I apply this?

I wanted as much confirmation as I could get that this it was God's will for me to be in vocational ministry. My prayers centered around 3 scriptures:

- *"And let the favor of the Lord our God be upon us; And do confirm for us the work of our hands; Yes, confirm the work of our hands."* Psalm 90:17
- *"Delight yourself in the LORD, and he will give you the desires of your heart."* Psalm 37:4
- *"You didn't choose me. I chose you. I appointed you to go and produce lasting fruit, so that the Father will give you whatever you ask for, using my name."* Jesus in John 15:16

After much seeking of God and talking to godly counselors I am wholeheartedly and unapologetically putting myself, my coaching services and my books out there. Granted the feelings are there sometimes, but I am not to walk by my feelings unless they match up to the truth.

What about you- if fear of charging for your products or services is holding you back from accomplishing your goals, what is the wrong belief?

_____
_____
_____
_____
_____
_____

"Obey God and leave all the consequences to Him." -Charles Stanley

"I'm not ready yet. I'm afraid of failure."

Paralysis by analysis, over-thinking, perfectionism and procrastination are all family members brought on by a fear of failure.

Ecclesiastes says *"If you wait for perfect conditions you'll never get anything done."* This verse is so liberating! Do you have a list of dreams and goals and things you believe the Lord is calling you to do? Perfect conditions will never come so don't wait for that.

Be excellent, yes of course, but don't let perfectionism hold you back.

Perfectionism can also lead to procrastination. When you are a perfectionist you can overthink something so much it leads you to paralysis by analysis. Which then leads to procrastination and waiting for deadlines so you have no choice but to just get it done.

You don't need to live that way!

It is truly God's grace that gives us the power to overcome perfectionism and to do the work He calls us to as imperfect as we may think we are. Listen to what Paul the apostle said in 1 Corinthians 15:10, *"But whatever I am now, it is all because God poured out his special favor on me—and not without results. For I have worked harder than any of the other* apostles; yet it was not I but God who was working through me by his grace."

So yes, we need to work hard, but not be a perfectionist and fall into "paralysis by analysis".

Are you holding back and being a perfectionist because you are afraid to put yourself out there for fear of what people may think? Be confident *"Just as water is turned into irrigation ditches, so the Lord directs the king's thoughts. He turns them wherever he wants to." Proverbs 21:1* God is working all things together for your good, so why worry?

The thoughts I battle coming from perfectionism are- *what if I put all this time into it and nothing comes of it? What if I am a terrible writer? What if I say the wrong thing and mislead someone biblically?*

Yet my deepest conviction is God is calling me to do this. That's all. I just need to obey.

Procrastination also comes to me when I have to do things I just don't like! There is no way around that. In this life we are going to have to do some things we don't like, Things that don't use our passions or strengths. His grace is sufficient. He will empower us in our weaknesses.

How do we conquer perfectionism and procrastination?

- **Don't overthink it.** *"For God is working in you, giving you the desire and the power to do what pleases him." Philippians 2:13*
- **Show up in the strength you have**: *"And God is able to make all grace abound to you, so that having all sufficiency in all things at all times, you may abound in every good work." 2 Corinthians 9:8*
- **Don't let fear or feelings make the decision-just do the next thing.** Break it down into manageable pieces, writing these down as your action plan. Then simply do the next thing.

"Start by doing what is necessary, then what is possible, and suddenly you are doing the impossible."-St. Francis of Assisi

Dealing with Negative Emotions

There can be times that you can't quite identify what the lie or the fear is that is holding you back. You just feel discouraged or defeated. Or maybe it's not a regular occurrence but rather you are just having a weird feeling that day.

We should look at negative emotions as the service engine soon light on our car dashboard. That generic light comes on when something needs attention. It's in those cases that we should bring the car to a mechanic who can diagnosis it and fix it. We don't just ignore it and risk the car breaking down. And so it is with our feelings. They are designed for a purpose and while we all enjoy the blessing of the positive emotions God has given us, it's important to bring the negative to our Creator to diagnosis and fix them.

Don't ignore the feeling, instead pause and ask God what is causing it. Wait and He will bring to your mind what thought or event is the cause.

For me there have been times I feel confused or down when I am trying to work and I know I need to stop and identify the source. Sometimes it could be that I have felt rejected or criticized and in my attempt to keep going, I've done just that- kept going instead of talking to God about it. Or maybe I have done something that hurt someone and I need to talk to God about it, confess it, receive His forgiveness and grace and then take that hard step and apologize and ask the person for forgiveness. Once I get to that root, I feel refreshed and can continue.

"Therefore if you are offering your gift at the altar and there remember that your brother has something against you, leave your gift there before the altar. First go and be reconciled to your brother; then come and offer your gift." Matthew 5:23-24

In what ways are you struggling with negative emotions?-

_____
_____
_____
_____
_____
_____

I encourage you don't push your negative feelings down but acknowledge them and give them to the Lord so you can move forward.

When you train yourself to do this in pursuit of the goal God has given you, you will be enabled to separate your emotions and simply take the steps that you have to. Fight the good fight of faith because you and I have an enemy that wants to steal, kill and destroy. Put on the full armor of God. Remember scripture is very specific about how we battle and conquer strongholds:

1. **The weapons of our warfare are not from earthly** wisdom but rather divine wisdom from God for His children.
2. **Pay attention to your thoughts.** Tear down any limited belief, lie, feeling of inadequacy or argument that contradicts God's truth and power. In this way you will bring it into captivity to the obedience of Christ.
3. **Instead of listening to yourself, talk to yourself!** Preach to yourself. Quote scripture out loud and yield that sword of the Spirit- God's Word.
4. **Overcome the accuser of the brethren, Satan.** We do this by knowing our sin is already covered by the blood of Jesus, the word of our testimony which includes our new identity and the purpose God has for us and the fact that we are trusting God with our lives.

Wrong Beliefs about God

What you believe about God shapes your entire life! Some people think He is judgmental with a list of do's and don'ts, ready and waiting to punish us. Others who had a bad earthly father think He is just like their dad. Some think He is uninterested in them as an individual. This wrong list goes on and on.

We learn from scripture who He truly is. Let me share just one scripture that God said about Himself as He passed in front of Moses when Moses asked to see His glory, *"Then the LORD passed by in front of him and proclaimed, "The LORD, the LORD God, compassionate and gracious, slow to anger, and abounding in lovingkindness and truth;" Exodus 34:6* Jesus also told Hs disciples in John 14:9, *"Anyone who has seen me has seen the Father!"*

Throughout both the Old and The New Testaments God/Jesus is revealing Himself and His attributes. An easy way to begin studying this is to read the gospels and listen to Jesus, see how He treated people, learn the way He responded and of His great love and truth. That is precisely how I fell in love with Him, I learned of His love for me personally.

Read a psalm a day as Gods attributes are revealed in relation to our struggles and our emotions. Read about the prodigal son and the Father and how that was a parable for our Heavenly Father and His reaction to our sin and our repentance.

Once I had a right understanding of who God was, it changed my life.

The biggest struggle I have ever had – a drug addiction was conquered once I learned and believed:
- What God said about Himself and His power
- What God said about me as His child

Let's look at an example of wrong beliefs about God in the parable of the talents Matthew 25:14-30

"Again, the Kingdom of Heaven can be illustrated by the story of a man going on a long trip. He called together his servants and entrusted his money to them while he was gone. He gave five bags of silver to one, two bags of silver to another, and one bag of silver to the last—dividing it in proportion to their abilities. He then left on his trip.

"The servant who received the five bags of silver began to invest the money and earned five more. The servant with two bags of silver also went to work and earned two more. But the servant who received the one bag of silver dug a hole in the ground and hid the master's money.

"After a long time, their master returned from his trip and called them to give an account of how they had used his money. The servant to whom he had entrusted the five bags of silver came forward with five more and said, 'Master, you gave me five bags of silver to invest, and I have earned five more.'

"The master was full of praise. 'Well done, my good and faithful servant. You have been faithful in handling this small amount, so now I will give you many more responsibilities. Let's celebrate together!'

"The servant who had received the two bags of silver came forward and said, 'Master, you gave me two bags of silver to invest, and I have earned two more.'

"The master said, 'Well done, my good and faithful servant. You have been faithful in handling this small amount, so now I will give you many more responsibilities. Let's celebrate together!'

"Then the servant with the one bag of silver came and said, 'Master, I knew you were a harsh man, harvesting crops you didn't plant and gathering crops you didn't cultivate. I was afraid I would lose your money, so I hid it in the earth. Look, here is your money back.'

"But the master replied, 'You wicked and lazy servant! If you knew I harvested crops I didn't plant and gathered crops I didn't cultivate, why didn't you deposit my money in the bank? At least I could have gotten some interest on it.'

"Then he ordered, 'Take the money from this servant, and give it to the one with the ten bags of silver. To those who use well what they are given, even more will be given, and they will have an abundance. But from those who do nothing, even what little they have will be taken away."

There are many lessons we can take from this parable but I'm just going to focus on the consequences of right and wrong beliefs about God. (The Master represents God in this story.)

Lesson 1: God is Good
- He willingly gives us everything we have and expects us to be good managers or wise stewards of it. *Logically, the fact that He expects that means He has also given us everything we need to do it well.*

- He divides what we are given in proportion to our abilities that He has graced us with. He doesn't question whether we are able to or not. He never expects us to do something that He will not enable us to do.

- He is generous and wants us to succeed. Like a good Father He wants to see us being wise and faithful with all He gives us. That is true success.

The first two servants had a reverence and a respect for their Master and didn't question Him, but notice the last servant regarded Him as a "harsh man" and used the excuse that he was afraid of losing His money so he did nothing.

But the Master makes a good point, if the servant did indeed view him that way and was afraid to lose the money then wouldn't he have at least kept it safe in the bank to accrue interest? Remember the definition earlier about an excuse just being a lie stuffed in the skin of a reason?

The Master spoke the truth in calling him a wicked and lazy servant and taking all he had away from Him. This servant obviously had a wrong belief and his wrong belief led to wrong behaviors. The other two servants had right beliefs and it inspired them to be wise stewards, to overcome whatever fear or doubt they may have had and to simply obey the task the Master had given them. **They were more concerned about pleasing the Master than they were of failure.**

Lesson 2: When you can be trusted, more is given to you.

Did you notice what the Master then did with the lazy servant's money? *"Then he ordered, 'Take the money from this servant, and give it to the one with the ten bags of silver. To those who use well what they are given, even more will be given, and they will have an abundance. But from those who do nothing, even what little they have will be taken away."*

Take a moment and ask God (who is more than happy to answer this):

- What are some of the things I am not wisely managing? Time? Spiritual gifts and talents? Money? Health? Relationships? What else has God entrusted to you that you know you need to be a better steward of? Journal a prayer to God about this.

_____

_____

_____

_____

_____

_____

_____

_____

_____

_____

_____

_____

_____

_____

_____

_____

- What do you need more of right now in your life?

_____
_____
_____
_____
_____
_____
_____
_____
_____
_____
_____

- Knowing that you will receive more of what you steward well, what can you do to be intentional and faithful?

_____
_____
_____
_____
_____
_____
_____
_____
_____
_____
_____
_____

"Give, and it will be given to you. Good measure, pressed down, shaken together, running over, will be put into your lap. For with the measure you use it will be measured back to you." Luke 6:38

CHAPTER 4

OBSTACLES & HINDRANCES

Obstacles & Hindrances

What about the external circumstances that have challenged and hindered your progress? Here are the most common ones I hear:

1. I don't have enough money
2. I don't have enough time
3. I don't have any help
4. I forgot what the goals were
5. Naysayers, Detractors & Critics
6. Productivity versus Activity

"I don't have enough money."

We could all say this and there are definitely times this seems like the truth. But here is a good time to introduce to you something that has helped me immensely over the years. It's distinguishing the facts from the truth.

The facts, well they are the facts. But the truth, Jesus is the truth, the Word of God is the truth, His promises are truth. Let me illustrate.

The facts:
Jesus was betrayed by His friend. He was sold for thirty pieces of silver. One of His best friends denied knowing Him. He was tortured beyond what you or I can imagine and God the Father completely forsook Him momentarily. He was hung on a cross, naked, and died a slow agonizing death. People who loved Him dearly watched this and stood by hopelessly and even though He had predicted His resurrection it seems no one was hoping for that or even remembered that. All they saw was pure evil and hopelessness, pure darkness and intense pain and grief. Those are the facts.

The Truth:
This was a rescue mission. This event saved you and I for all of eternity, bringing us into a right and glorious relationship with our Father and Creator. To those who have put their trust in the finished work of Jesus

Christ, the penalty and the power of sin has been taken care of. This was God's purpose in the midst of the pain. What was the darkness day in history was the day Jesus publicly triumphed against Satan and his demons, the day that Jesus crushed the head of the serpent, the day that all the power of our sin and the penalty for our sin was willingly taken by our Savior. The day He cried out "It is finished."

That is the beautiful truth!

So what could the truth be in not having enough money to accomplish goals? Here are some thoughts on the truth. The truth is our *God owns the cattle on a thousand hills*, meaning He owns everything- (Psalm 50:10). He is all loving, all knowing and all powerful. He wants what is best for us. He will provide for us, for our needs. That is a promise. He is sovereign and He knows best for each of us personally.

In my new career I have yet to make what I was making previously. I have had to fight discouragement missing my old paychecks! And yet, there have been more blessings than ever. I get to do what I love and get paid for it. I get to work from home. I get to make my own schedule. And honestly, He has provided every step of the way.

Even with that, my goal is still to exceed what I used to make. I've walked with Jesus long enough to know and trust, it's just a matter of time. What if more money right now means I miss out on God's best for me? Or accomplish something that was never really God's will for me? Or miss out on being dependent on Him in a way that my relationship and intimacy with Him grows in a way it couldn't otherwise? How could I see Him work in amazing ways if I wasn't looking for His hand?

"For the LORD God is a sun and shield: the LORD will give grace and glory: no good thing will he withhold from them that walk uprightly." Psalm 84:11

I hate to admit this but there is also a biblical principle at work right now as well. In many ways I have been foolish with money, and not faithful with little. Maybe that is your story too. Thankfully, He promises to provide for all our needs regardless of our actions simply because we are His children. We can count on Romans 8:28, *"all things work together for good to those who love Him and are called according to His purpose."* So even if we are responsible for the lack of money He will use it for good.

We don't always like to hear it but our holiness and our faithfulness and our trust in Him is much more important to God. He has a big calling for us so we have to be faithful! And like a good father He really is faithful to discipline us (not punish us) so we can get on track and enjoy everything He has for us.

"God's discipline is always good for us, so that we might share in his holiness. No discipline is enjoyable while it is happening—it's painful! But afterward there will be a peaceful harvest of right living for those who are trained in this way." Hebrews 12:10-11

God can make a way
Regardless of the reason for the lack of money, God can make a way where there seems to be no way. Actually, He specializes in that. Remember the Red Sea? If it's His will for your life, He will make a way!

- **Be faithful with little**. If in the last chapter money was something God brought to your mind to be a better steward of, then surrender to His will. As Mary, Jesus' mother said at the wedding feast when Jesus was going to turn water into wine, *"Do what He tells you."*
- **Remember the harvest principle.** *"Let us not become weary in doing good, for at the proper time we will reap a harvest if we do not give up." Galatians 6:9*

There is a time for preparing the soil, sowing the seed and watering the seed. The farmer is not surprised by this truth. Why should we be? A farmer doesn't plant a seed today and expect to see the crop tomorrow. Instead he does what needs to be done daily trusting the harvest is coming. So don't grow weary. Don't give up. Keep walking by faith, not focusing on your lack but focusing on His ability and abundance.

"Good planning and hard work lead to prosperity, but hasty shortcuts lead to poverty." Proverbs 21:5

"I don't have enough time."

It's been said if you are too busy for God then you are too busy. I think the same can be said for the goals God gives us. If you are too busy to accomplish them, then you are too busy. He is not going to give us goals to be done in a certain season and not provide the time. It's up to us how we spend it.

There are definitely seasons in our life when we are busier than other times. This is why it's important to understand what God's priority for our lives are in each season, so we know what to say yes to and what to say no to. That truly is the battle- being intentional about how we spend our time while remaining flexible to God's divine appointments. You can always make more money but you cannot make more time.

I've been in the position where I worked at least 40 hours a week, had a household to run and had goals outside of work. It can be hard when you feel like the best of your energy and time is spent by the time you get home. That is how many Americans feel so they become complacent and unwind by watching TV all evening after work. No judgment here- I have my Netflix binges and sometimes that is exactly what I need to do and just recharge. But many times the time slots that we can use to accomplish our goals are before or after work. We have all been given 24 hours a day. Those who are successful in their goals usually don't have less to do, they just use their time more wisely.

"So be careful how you act; these are difficult days. Don't be fools; be wise: make the most of every opportunity you have for doing good. [17] Don't act thoughtlessly but try to find out and do whatever the Lord wants you to." Ephesians 5:15-17

How do we fit in our personal time with the Lord, housecleaning, exercise, cooking and homework with the kids? I truly believe it comes from an attitude of gratitude and a sense of purpose. When we realize how short time really is and that we need to enjoy every moment we will be more intentional about not wasting time and living with mediocrity.

When something is important to you and is from God, you will be energized. It may not happen until you are right there in the moment but it will happen. It consistently happens that God will give me a second wind and focus when I am doing something He has called me to do. When I served in the drug and alcohol ministry my day would start at 5am and I wouldn't get back home until 9pm. But as soon as I'd get to church, my energy would flow, God would give me the wisdom, the words and the compassion to glorify him and help others. It really felt supernatural every time. I am not advocating however being a Martha and not a Mary. If my schedule including "serving Jesus" became too crowded and pulled me away from the one thing Jesus called best, spending time at His feet learning from Him, then serving would have to be let go of.

There is a time to be a Martha and a time to be a Mary.

"Now as they went on their way, Jesus entered a village. And a woman named Martha welcomed him into her house. And she had a sister called Mary, who sat at the Lord's feet and listened to his teaching. But Martha was distracted with all her serving. She came over and said, "Lord, don't you care that my sister has left me to serve alone? Tell her to help me." But the Lord answered her, "Martha, Martha, you are anxious and troubled about many things, but one thing is necessary. Mary has chosen the good portion, which will not be taken away from her."

Luke 10:38-42

Balance and rhythm are important concepts to consider. We all think the goal is work/life balance. If you believe you just need more balance then when your schedule isn't balanced you may fall under condemnation and hopelessness and give up on your goals. I am not saying you shouldn't work on balance, it is important but what you and I both need more than balance is to understand the season so we can stay in God's perfect peace.

The bible talks about seasons. *"For everything there is a season, and a time for every matter under heaven: a time to be born, and a time to die; a time to plant, and a time to pluck up what is planted; a time to kill, and a time to heal; a time to break down, and a time to build up; a time to weep, and a time to laugh; a time to mourn, and a time to dance; a time to cast away stones, and a time to gather stones together; a time to embrace, and a time to refrain from embracing; ..." Ecclesiastes 3:1-8*

It could be an amazing, happy season, a difficult season, or a season of hard work. Maybe you are a new mother, maybe you are just starting a business, maybe your business is booming, maybe your ministry is growing, maybe you are grieving the loss of loved one, maybe you are in the midst of a sickness, or you are taking care of a family member. There is no way you can compartmentalize your life, nor should you. **You need to go with the flow, with the rhythm of this season.** Some things will have to be put on the backburner, even just temporally without anger, guilt, frustration, or trying to do everything and failing miserably. You only have so much bandwidth so you must prioritize.

"Blessed is the one who does not walk in step with the wicked or stand in the way that sinners take or sit in the company of mockers, but whose delight is in the law of the LORD, and who meditates on his law day and night. That person is like a tree planted by streams of water, **which yields its fruit in season and whose leaf does not wither—whatever they do prospers."** Psalm 1:1-3

6 years ago, I took a step of faith and quit my fulltime job. I believed and still believe that was what God was calling me to do. During those 6 years I have been in a season of building a business; really focusing on walking in the call God has on my life all while keeping money coming in and being a good wife and daughter, friend, business person and coach. Yet, life still happens. Trials and tribulations. In the midst I have endured strain in my marriage because of our lower income. I was diagnosed with fibromyalgia. My brother unexpectedly died. And we adopted a deaf puppy with separation anxiety. It's truly been the most difficult season of my adult life second only to my drug addiction and my dad dying season.

God's grace got me through and I am now at the point where my fibromyalgia is healed, my grief (although still there) is not acute but rather I have the sweet peace of God covering me as the tears flow, and my deaf puppy is now a 4 years old, obedient, well-adjusted and sweet guy.

And then last October I got in a car accident. I was not seriously injured but injured enough that for 6 months I have had to spend about 10 hours a week going to doctor and physical therapy appointments. That's a lot of time. I have been very frustrated, angry in fact that so much of my time was being taken from me through no fault of my own. I have things to do!

I have had to continually bring my disappointment and stress before the Lord remembering He is in control, He knows, He cares and *all things are working together for my good*. I also have to recognize when I am angry about not accomplishing something I think I need to, I must give that very thing to the Lord and not allow it to become an idol. It's hard! As I write this I am 6 months behind the schedule I set for completing this book. But am I really? Did God need to teach me something that He wanted in the book? Perhaps.

God's timing is not always ours. His ways are not our ways.

"For my thoughts are not your thoughts, neither are your ways my ways," declares the LORD. "As the heavens are higher than the earth, so are my ways higher than your ways and my thoughts than your thoughts." Isaiah 55:8-9

"Expectations minus reality equals disappointment."
Randy Carlson

Right now, I have less time for socializing, leisurely lunches, and long phone calls. But it's not forever. As long as I get my time with the Lord and my husband and mom, my work and serving and remain open to "divine interruptions" aka appointments, then I will be maintaining my priorities in this season.

"Go to the ant, O sluggard; consider her ways, and be wise. Without having any chief, officer, or ruler, she prepares her bread in summer and gathers her food in harvest." Proverbs 6:6-8

I have had to put boundaries in place and not allow others to make me feel bad because I'm not trying to balance and do everything.

- *"If I partake with thankfulness, why am I denounced because of that for which I give thanks? So, whether you eat or drink, or whatever you do, do all to the glory of God." 1 Corinthians 10:30-31*
- *"You will keep in perfect peace all who trust in You, all whose thoughts are fixed on You!" Isaiah 26:3*

What season are you in right now?

_____
_____
_____
_____
_____
_____
_____
_____
_____

What's your rhythm?

First, let's define rhythm. Oxford dictionary defines it as: *A strong, regular repeated pattern of movement or sound; a regularly recurring sequence of events or processes.*

Have you noticed that certain hours or days make it much easier to find the flow where you are extra productive, lost in the moment and accomplish more in one sitting than you would at a different time?

That is because we all have our own natural rhythm. Don't take the so-called expert's opinions for what a successful person's schedule looks like but ask God to show you. Study yourself and your own energy cycles.

For example, most success coaches advise their clients to exercise first thing in the morning so that it gets done. While I agree exercise is definitely a daily priority and priorities should be done before the day gets away from you, I myself intentionally schedule it a little differently because of my natural rhythm.

When I get up in the morning I have the most energy, mental clarity and creativity of the day. My mind is brimming with strategies, thoughts and ideas, things I want to write about, marketing plans, interior decorating and color ideas. So, I enjoy my quiet time with Lord, my bible and my journal in the morning with my coffee and then I can get into my flow, my creativity, my action steps for my making my business goals.

Mornings **I try not to** schedule anything with clients or other people or anything outside of my home office for that matter. That includes phone calls.

In a perfect world I would exercise at lunchtime or early afternoon. (But because I prefer group classes, I am at the mercy of the studio's schedule.)

People energize me so meetings and phone calls are better for me in the afternoon as I don't need the mental clarity, it'll naturally come. It's tried and true that even if I don't feel like I have the energy for meetings with clients or to work out, I always get physical energy for these things as I enjoy them so much.

In the evening, perfection is dinner, spending time with my husband usually watching Netflix, taking a bath (in the winter), reading, and going to bed at a reasonable hour. That is my perfect natural rhythm.

Does it always happen? No, which I can struggle with, experiencing irritation and resentment when it doesn't go my way (which again is a good way to reveal an idol). I battle those bad attitudes by taking my thoughts captive to the obedience of Christ Jesus.

I will intentionally consider my boundaries and pray for discernment as to whether I am being a people pleaser and violating my boundaries or question is it a divine appointment. If I have violated my boundaries rather than beat myself up or resent others, I receive God's grace. And if it's a divine appointment I look to what is unseen and rejoice at God's providence. If I blow it and rebel against what I know God wants me to do I receive His grace. No matter what the case is I cannot dwell on it in an unhealthy way but instead:

- I need to accept the valuable lesson that is working together for my good.
- I need to not be such a control freak in some areas and in some areas, I need to be a wiser steward.
- Always I need to remember His burden is light and His yoke is easy. It's about relationship with Him not religion and legalism.

"Are you tired? Worn out? Burned out on religion? Come to me. Get away with me and you'll recover your life. I'll show you how to take a real rest. Walk with me and work with me—watch how I do it. Learn the unforced rhythms of grace. I won't lay anything heavy or ill-fitting on you. Keep company with me and you'll learn to live freely and lightly." Jesus in Matthew 11:28-30

Ask God to reveal to you how you can better get in sync with your natural rhythm and His rhythm.

_____
_____
_____
_____
_____

What would your perfect day look like?

_____
_____
_____
_____
_____
_____
_____

What would your perfect week look like?

_____
_____
_____
_____
_____
_____
_____

"I don't have any help."

This is a common reason I hear from women on why they are struggling to achieve their goals. I am not denying that help is not necessary and if everyone would just pitch in around the house then you'd have a better chance of accomplishing your goals. What I want to point out here is that it is unrealistic to expect that and it is not a good reason for not accomplishing what God has promised to empower you for.

I want you to change your mindset. It's great if everyone pitches in but not necessary to accomplish your calling. I also want you to ask God to open your eyes to the help He has sent through other people and other means. If it is necessary God will indeed send you someone to help you directly.

He saw it was *"not good"* for man to be alone when He looked at Adam. His word also tells us not to *"forsake the assembling with one another"* and that *"He comforts us in all our troubles so that we can comfort others."* Its clear God has made us brothers and sisters in Christ and that we are to be a family. With that being said, it is still all the glory to God. He alone is the Provider, the One we count on and trust to *"supply all our needs"*.

He will do it in the most perfect way giving us exactly what our soul needs.

If we stay stuck because we don't see the help we think we need, we will end up in the "expectations minus reality equals disappointment" mode. But here is one of God's promises to you:

"God is able to make all grace abound toward you, that you, always having all sufficiency in all things, may have abundance for every good work." 2 Corinthians 9:8

Let's look at an example from scripture.

"... Jesus went up to Jerusalem. Now there is in Jerusalem by the Sheep Gate a pool, which is called in Hebrew, Bethesda, having five porches. In these lay a great multitude of sick people, blind, lame, paralyzed, waiting

for the moving of the water. For an angel went down at a certain time into the pool and stirred up the water; then whoever stepped in first, after the stirring of the water, was made well of whatever disease he had. Now a certain man was there who had an infirmity thirty-eight years. When Jesus saw him lying there, and knew that he already had been in that condition a long time. He said to him, **"Do you want to be made well?" The sick man answered Him, "Sir, I have no man to put me into the pool when the water is stirred up; but while I am coming, another steps down before me."** *Jesus said to him, "Rise, take up your bed and walk." And immediately the man was made well, took up his bed, and walked." John 5:1-8*

Jesus didn't ask *why* this man hadn't been made well. He asked if he wanted to be made well. Yet the man responds to the question and says he had no one to help him, clearly disappointed and discouraged. In the end all he needed was Jesus.

I personally have found the greatest breakthroughs in life when no one was helping me.

"You may never know that JESUS is all you need, until JESUS is all you have." Corrie ten Boom

"I look up to the mountains—does my help come from there? My help comes from the LORD, who made heaven and earth! He will not let you stumble; the one who watches over you will not slumber." Psalm 121:1-3

Jesus has a plan and a purpose for you. It's actually too big for you. It's no surprise your reaction in the natural will be that you need help. It's true. You do. You need Him and He chooses what that help will look like.

When I got clean from drugs, God sent me one person who was speaking to me about Jesus and the gospel of grace. She was a drug addict herself. She was God's answer to my prayer and told me the things God knew I needed to hear. After a heavy duty, six-year drug addiction and a lifetime of recreational drug and alcohol use, the Lord set me free without rehab, without a sponsor, without meetings or counseling, without an accountability partner. But He used this drug addicted friend who knew the Word of God and He used the pastors with radio ministries.

Other times I have accomplished goals surrounded by lots of encouraging people. For instance, my main fitness routine is in a group class. I love the high standard that is set in a group class. Left to my own, when the exercise gets tough and my muscles are shaking I would probably quit. But surrounded by other like-minded tough women, I embrace the shake and stay in it.

He really does know what kind of help we need. Just ask.

- *"Much is required from those to whom much is given, for their responsibility is greater." Luke 12:48*
- *"In fact, we expected to die. But as a result, we stopped relying on ourselves and learned to rely only on God, who raises the dead." 2 Corinthians 1:9*
- *"He alone is my rock and my salvation, my fortress where I will not be shaken. My victory and honor come from God alone." Psalm 62:6-7*
- *"It is better to take refuge in the Lord than to trust in people." Psalm 118:8*

"I forgot my goals"

This is by far the easiest hindrance out of all of them to overcome. I'm just as guilty though. When I worked in sales and marketing I had a quota and written goals and action plans were mandatory for every quarter and annually. (Employers know the power of written goals and a plan!)

Then there were years that I didn't write out my personal or self-employment goals. Then there was the year I wrote them in my journal and didn't read them again until the following year when I reviewing my journal. And guess what? I veered off in other directions instead of staying on course. I now keep my goals written and right in front of me every day and even talk to God about them every day so I stay very intentional.

- Write them down
- Keep them in front of you daily
- Pray about them continually

And the LORD answered me, and said, 'Write the vision, and make it plain on tables, that he may run that reads it.' Habakkuk 2:2

Naysayers, Detractors and Critics

This is tough one as these are outside forces speaking into your life and sadly, many times they are close to you. You need to have a plan on how to deal with these people so you can get that backbone that will stand and push through trusting in God.

I was very fortunate that growing up my parents encouraged me and made me believe I could do whatever I put my mind to. They recognized my strengths and talents and affirmed me. I always did well in school so I had that same support from my teachers. I grew up confident in who I was and what I could do. But then I became a drug addict. In my fruitless efforts to get clean apart from Christ I learned I really could not (in my own power) do anything I set my mind to. That was a very valuable lesson.

The good news is, *"I can do all things through Christ who strengthens me."* *Philippians 4:13* and *Philippians 4:13,* *"For God is working in you, giving you the desire and the power to do what pleases him."* Anything that God calls us to do, we are guaranteed His power and provision.

Sadly, there are negative people- naysayers, detractors and critics. If they don't know the Lord or don't trust in His power and purpose they can be blinded.

Naysayers- *person who habitually expresses negative or pessimistic views: one who denies, refuses, opposes, or is skeptical or cynical about something*

Detractors- *a person who belittles or disparages someone or something*

Critics- *one given to harsh or captious judgment*

The first time I was involved with someone like this, it nearly broke me. I valued this person's opinions. I didn't even know how to handle the negativity and the critical spirit. I had no prior experience (thankfully) and was very vulnerable to the attacks. I will say there is a right and healthy way to cope and also a wrong, unhealthy way to cope. **You do get to choose.**

I don't know who has criticized or discouraged you-if it was your parents or family, if you were a child or if it is someone currently in your life, but Jesus knows. He cares. He knows the talents, skills, gifts and calling on your life and His word is the last word.

Take Heart
You and I are actually in good company having these naysayers. As always, the bible is very relevant to this. We already saw that Joshua and Caleb were outnumbered by naysayers and as such had to wait 40 years to get into he promised land. Let's look at a couple more examples.

David- In the famous battle of David and Goliath, we know David conquers the giant. God was with him and had called him to do it. It was a big calling. An impossible one. But David's courage and confidence were in the Lord alone, not in his own strength.

Let's back up a little in the story. Listen to this conversation that took place before David accomplished killing Goliath. *"David asked the men standing near him, "What will be done for the man who kills this Philistine and removes this disgrace from Israel? Who is this uncircumcised Philistine that he should defy the armies of the living God?" They repeated to him what they had been saying and told him, "This is what will be done for the man who kills him. "When Eliab, David's oldest brother, heard him speaking with the men, he burned with anger at him and asked, "Why have you come down here? And with whom did you leave those few sheep in the wilderness? I know how conceited you are and how wicked your heart is; you came down only to watch the battle." "Now what have I done?" said David. "Can't I even speak?" 1 Samuel 17:26-29*

Talk about a naysayer! His own brother, Eliab who should know him so well accuses him of being conceited and having a wicked heart! That was not true. And from the outside looking in we can see Eliab was probably just jealous. Or maybe not. Maybe he projected on David his own shortcomings assuming that like him, David was conceited and wicked. Only God knows the thoughts and intents of a man. Never-the-less this had to hurt. It had to be discouraging.

We see from David's response, *"Now what have I done?" said David. "Can't I even speak?"* that this was not the first time he'd been attacked and accused by his brother.

How did he handle it? *"He then turned away to someone else and brought up the same matter, and the men answered him as before."* 1 Samuel 17:30

The vision I have of this exchange makes me laugh. He simply turned away and spoke to someone else more reasonable. It rolled right off his back. What a healthy way to cope. And he went on to kill Goliath, get great riches, marry the Kings daughter and pay no taxes. It blessed the people of Israel, it glorified God and brought David blessings. Success!

Nehemiah- Nehemiah had a burden on his heart from those coming home to Jerusalem from captivity. Jerusalem was in ruins and the wall around the city needed to be rebuilt. He loved God and loved the people so he prayed for God to allow him to go rebuild. God answered his prayer, gave him favor and the work began, but not without his share of detractors.

"When Sanballat heard that we were rebuilding the wall, he became angry and was greatly incensed. He ridiculed the Jews, and in the presence of his associates and the army of Samaria, he said, "What are those feeble Jews doing? Will they restore their wall? Will they offer sacrifices? Will they finish in a day? Can they bring the stones back to life from those heaps of rubble—burned as they are?" Tobiah the Ammonite, who was at his side, said, "What they are building—even a fox climbing up on it would break down their wall of stones!" Nehemiah 4:1-3

Nehemiah knew that he knew that he knew that God had sent him. His response was to give this right back to God through prayer.
"Hear us, our God, for we are despised. Turn their insults back on their own heads. Give them over as plunder in a land of captivity. Do not cover up their guilt or blot out their sins from your sight, for they have thrown insults in the face of the builders.
So we rebuilt the wall till all of it reached half its height, for the people worked with all their heart." Nehemiah 4:4-6

But the detractors were not done trying.

"When word came to Sanballat, Tobiah, Geshem the Arab and the rest of our enemies that I had rebuilt the wall and not a gap was left in it— though up to that time I had not set the doors in the gates— Sanballat and Geshem sent me this message: "Come, let us meet together in one of the villages on the plain of Ono." But they were scheming to harm me; so I sent messengers to them with this reply: "I am carrying on a great project and cannot go down. Why should the work stop while I leave it and go down to you?" Four times they sent me the same message, and each time I gave them the same answer." Nehemiah 6:1-4

This time we don't hear Nehemiah's prayer although throughout the book he makes every move covered in prayer so I am sure there was prayer about this. No doubt God had somehow revealed to Nehemiah that these men were scheming to harm him. His answer was no. Four times they asked and his resolve stayed firm. No.

There are many lessons we can take away from this as we pursue what God has called us to do. We've already talked about people pleasing and boundaries but we didn't talk about it in the context of those who oppose you.

Be Discerning. Have you ever tried to win someone over that didn't like you? There is a time and a place for that. Abraham Lincoln said, "Do I not destroy my enemies when I make them my friends?" In this case Nehemiah knew that these people were evil. They did not want what God wanted. They were not going to change their minds and be his friends. They were sent by the enemy to harm him. Christian, you are not a doormat. Please care more about what God wants you to do than trying to win over everyone.

Pray for wisdom and discernment so that you are not deceived.

The enemy of best is good. Let's just say for arguments sake that they were not sent to harm him but just had some questions or wanted to get to know him or wanted to partner with him on something. This may be a more probable situation in your life. It certainly is in my life. I have many opportunities to get involved in the business community. I have been on the boards of a few organizations and on committees of other ones. When I was in my previous position those were strategic ways of building your clientele and keeping top of mind with potential clients. But that was then when I worked for a business publication. In my current season, it is a good thing but it's not the best. Let the peace of God rule in your heart. When you know that you need to be focused on the thing God called you to do, be aware distractions will come your way.

If you stand for nothing you'll fall for anything.

Let your no be no. There are those who will try to wear you down. Nehemiah had to say no four times!

"Behold, I am sending you out as sheep in the midst of wolves, so be wise as serpents and innocent as doves." Matthew 10:16

Don't give up

We can read story after story in the bible of great opposition towards God's people and the successful accomplishment of the calling on their lives.

We can also look to more current examples of people who were resolute in their pursuit of their dreams in the midst of opposition.

Walt Disney was denied bank financing 300 times. He was also fired by a newspaper editor because he "lacked imagination and had no good ideas."

Dr Seuss was rejected by publishers 27 times.

After a performance Elvis Presley was told by the concert hall manager he would be better off going back to driving trucks.

Van Gogh whose paintings are now worth millions of dollars, sold only one of his paintings while he was alive to a friend for a small amount of money.

One of the most important lessons we should take away from these stories is that insults and opposition do not mean we should quit! Don't allow yourself to take on a victim mentality. You are more than an overcomer! Keep your eyes on Jesus and your hand on the plow moving forward.

Accuser of the Brethren

It is important to remember that Satan will influence people around us to speak his accusations and criticism to stop God's work and hurt us. Ephesians 6:10 tells us, *"For our struggle is not against flesh and blood, but against the rulers, against the authorities, against the powers of this dark world and against the spiritual forces of evil in the heavenly realms."*

Our battle is not against those people but against demons who are doing battle against us in the spiritual realm. When you realize that you can then fight the right battle by freely forgiving the people who don't know what they are doing and continue on with doing what God is calling you to do **by putting on the full armor of God**.

"Finally, be strong in the Lord and in his mighty power. [11] Put on the full armor of God, so that you can take your stand against the devil's schemes." Ephesians 6:10-11

"The tongue has the power of life and death..." Proverbs 18:21

Words can build up or they can tear down.

According to a Harvard Business Review study, the highest performing teams had a ratio of 6 positive comments to 1 negative.

According to Dr. Henry Cloud, a Christian, psychologist and leadership expert, it takes 7 compliments to make up for 1 insult.

Dr. Caroline Leaf, a Christian and a cognitive neuroscientist who has done extensive research claims that 75% to 95% of the illnesses that plague us today are a direct result of our thought life.

You can see why Satan would try and harm and stop you by those speaking negative. Before you despair remember God is sovereign and can certainly override any human statistic. Statistics simply don't trump God's promises. Listen to God.

"The LORD your God is in your midst, a mighty one who will save; he will rejoice over you with gladness; he will quiet you by his love; he will exult over you with loud singing." Zephaniah 3:17

How can you overcome?

Course Correction
While all the examples we have looked at have been untrue accusations of naysayers, detractors and critics there are times where God is really bringing about course correction.

Receiving constructive criticism from a person who is full of grace, an effective communicator and a person who you value their opinion can be easy. Just think about a doctor or a personal trainer or a life coach that you hire. You are paying them for course correction and you readily receive it.

But how about those people who come across as harsh and judgmental? Let's face it, there are those people who think they are perfect and love to give unsolicited advice! Perhaps they are saying things that you already know or have already tried. Or maybe they like to use those words "you never..." or "you always..." It's easy to think they are speaking for Satan and disregard and reject what they have to say.

One of the most valuable lessons we can learn is not to take it personally and actually consider what is being said. I also make it a point to pray for that person that they would mature in their communication skills and THINK before they speak:

T- it is true?
H- is it helpful?
I- is it inspiring?
N- is it necessary?
K- is it kind?

But until Jesus comes back, there are going to be those who don't think before they speak and it can even be us! So, we need to be proactive.

"Instead, we will **speak the truth in love,** *growing in every way more and more like Christ, who is the head of his body, the church." Ephesians 4:15*

Receive, Reject or Redeem

We are told that we are to *"take our thoughts captive to the obedience of Christ Jesus"* (2 Corinthians 10:5) so naturally we should also do the same with the words that are spoken to us.

If you are walking circumspectly, sensitive to the Holy Spirit, open to His leading so you can walk in His perfect will and plan, then you should be expecting course correction. Keep that in mind always so you can simply respond to others instead of reacting.

I first heard of Receive, Reject or Redeem from Pastor Mark Driscoll. He used it in a little different way- focusing on how a Christian should engage culture. We will use it to filter the harsh, judgmental comments of a critic and poor communicator.

Receive- Is what this person saying something that would be a good, beneficial course of action. Receive it.

Reject: Is this completely a lie, an attack on you with no redeeming qualities? Reject it. Bring the hurt it causes you directly to God. Pray for tough skin and a tender heart. Forgive them and move forward.

Redeem: Maybe it's not true, but there is something you can take away from it and be better for it. Redeem it. Bring the hurt it causes you directly to God. Forgive them and move forward implementing whatever course correction God has revealed to you.

"Don't say anything that would hurt another person. Instead, speak only what is good so that you can give help wherever it is needed. That way, what you say will help those who hear you." Ephesians 4:29

"The wounds of a friend are faithful, but the kisses of an enemy are deceitful." Proverbs 27:6

Be Proactive with Truth & Life-Giving Thoughts
We should be diligent about maintaining our peace and knowing our value as Children of God and our identity in Him. Our significance comes from Him and our relationship to Him alone, not from our accomplishments or our talents or strengths. Those are great but we are now Saint's. We are New Creations in Christ. We are Ambassadors for Christ. We are a Royal

Priesthood. Chosen, adopted, redeemed, accepted, equipped, loved. You are completely unique, beautiful and cherished in His eyes, He is pleased with His you. You are clean and set apart in Christ. He delights in you. Remind yourself and the spiritual realm out loud who you are in Christ!

Don't forsake the assembling with other Believers. If you are spending a lot of time in the world with people who think differently than you and/or with critical people, it'll take a toll on you. You need to have a person or a group that you do life with, friends that can speak into your life and pray with you.

Make sure you have people in your midst that are where you want to be. Surrounding ourselves with people who are more successful in any area of life is good for us. It's been said you are the sum of the 5 people you spend the most time with. Make sure you choose to spend time with people who are at the level you want to be at in all areas of life. And you should be that person for someone else and help them grow as well.

I also supplement spending time with people with listening to sermons and podcasts and reading books that inspire and encourage me in the areas that God is growing and working on in my life.

- **Saturate your mind in scripture.** You will then know the truth and the truth will set you free. You will be readily able to take your thoughts captive and to yield your Sword of the Spirit.
- **Ask God to send people to give you encouragement and feedback**. Ask Him to even out that positive to negative ratio. He knows what you need to hear. I have done this on many occasions and He never ceases to amaze me how He answers that prayer!
- **Ponder those life-giving truths that have been spoken to you**. Replace, replace, replace.
- If you are the one putting yourself down, **learn to talk truth to yourself, not listen to yourself, your fears or failures or Satan**. Many times, we think these negative thoughts are ours, but they are really coming from the evil one who is a liar and wants to destroy you.

"Gracious words are like a honeycomb, sweetness to the soul and health to the body." Proverbs 16:24

Productivity verses Activity

When it comes to accomplishing goals understanding the difference between activity and productivity is crucial. Have you ever had a super busy day but really accomplished nothing of importance? We all have. Sometimes there is just no way around it and the "tyranny of the urgent" pushes out the important stuff.

A great illustration of this concept is the story of the walnuts and the rice. The story goes that a professor wanted to show his students how to prioritize. He took an empty jar, a handful of walnuts and a bag of rice. The goal was to fit it all in the jar.

When he put the rice in first, he could not fit the walnuts. However, when he started with the walnuts, although they came right up to the top of the jar, there were spaces throughout. He was then easily able to pour the rice in fitting it all in the jar. The moral of the story is that if you start with the most productive use of your time, the big things, your priorities, then the urgencies, the small activities that must be done will fit in accordingly.

We need to intentionally consider what are "walnuts" and what is "rice" so we are better able to adjust our schedules. You may need to let go of the things that are not the BEST use of your time. Or you may need to delegate or outsource.

Delegate- *entrust (a task or responsibility) to another person, typically one who is less senior than oneself.*

Outsource- *contract (work) out*

I think many times we just get so used to doing everything ourselves we don't even realize getting help through delegation or outsourcing is an option. Maybe it hasn't been modeled for us or maybe we think doing so would be selfish. But consider this: it not only helps you accomplish what you've been called to, it is a blessing for others to use their spiritual gifts, talents and skills. Delegate!

Delegation

We first see this in Moses life. He was one busy guy with a huge calling who would not have been able to accomplish the God sized calling he had on his life if he did learn to delegate. And the people would have missed out on their calling.

"When Moses' father-in-law saw all that Moses was doing for the people, he asked, "What are you really accomplishing here? Why are you trying to do all this alone while everyone stands around you from morning till evening?"

Moses replied, "Because the people come to me to get a ruling from God. When a dispute arises, they come to me, and I am the one who settles the case between the quarreling parties. I inform the people of God's decrees and give them his instructions."

"This is not good!" Moses' father-in-law exclaimed. "You're going to wear yourself out—and the people, too. This job is too heavy a burden for you to handle all by yourself. Now listen to me, and let me give you a word of advice, and may God be with you. You should continue to be the people's representative before God, bringing their disputes to him. Teach them God's decrees, and give them his instructions. Show them how to conduct their lives. But select from all the people some capable, honest men who fear God and hate bribes. Appoint them as leaders over groups of one thousand, one hundred, fifty, and ten. They should always be available to solve the people's common disputes, but have them bring the major cases to you. Let the leaders decide the smaller matters themselves. They will help you carry the load, making the task easier for you. If you follow this advice, and if God commands you to do so, then you will be able to endure the pressures, and all these people will go home in peace."

Moses listened to his father-in-law's advice and followed his suggestions."
Exodus 18:14-24

What a relief delegating had to be for Moses.
When I was doing ministry at the church I had an assistant for a couple of years and it was amazing! With her help I could focus more on the ladies and the teaching portion.

It should be a goal of all of ours this year to delegate more. If you don't have a team to delegate to, could you get an intern or could you outsource? Could you look at household duties and come up with a plan for everyone to work in their strengths to get the work done more efficiently?

Outsourcing
My husband and I recently outsourced our payroll and accounting. It has been a tremendous help as we pursue the duties and tasks that we are gifted at. Letting go of it also took a lot of strain off our marriage. But we had to be wise in our timing, as with most small businesses we had to grow to the place where it made financial sense to do so.

As I surround myself with successful, godly women who I want to learn and grow from, I have realized that several of them have outsourced their housecleaning to open up more hours for their family, their work and their ministry. Guess what one of my goals is this year!

Funny thing is even when I worked fulltime outside of the house and spent many hours away from home doing ministry I never considered hiring cleaning help. I could have afforded it. Instead I did it myself. When I mentioned that to one of the women they made a valid point; my mom (who is like Martha Stewart) always modeled for me a working woman who kept an impeccable house. I don't even remember friends having house cleaning help so to me it was a foreign concept, one not even on my radar. Yet, if I could budget for outsourcing I would be able to spend that time on things I know God is calling me to do.

I encourage you to be wise and discerning and seek God and godly counsel if you are considering delegating and outsourcing. Then act either through making it a goal with a plan or, if the timing is right taking the plunge into handing it off to someone.

"The little foxes are ruining the vineyards. Catch them, for the grapes are all in blossom." Song of Solomon 2:15

You can do all that God has called you to do but you've got to be intentional about it.

List the walnuts in your life:

_____
_____
_____
_____
_____
_____

List the rice in your life:

_____
_____
_____
_____
_____
_____

What are some ways you can be more productive?

_____
_____
_____
_____
_____
_____
_____
_____

Are there some activities you can delegate?

_____
_____
_____
_____
_____
_____
_____

Is there someone God is bringing to mind that you can delegate to?

_____
_____
_____
_____
_____
_____

Are there some activities you can outsource?

_____
_____
_____
_____
_____
_____
_____
_____
_____
_____
_____
_____

"Where is the man who fears the Lord? God will teach him how to choose the best." Psalm 25:12

CHAPTER 5

SPIRITUAL GIFTS

Living as Children of Light

"With the Lord's authority I say this: Live no longer as the Gentiles do, for they are hopelessly confused. Their minds are full of darkness; they wander far from the life God gives because they have closed their minds and hardened their hearts against him. They have no sense of shame. They live for lustful pleasure and eagerly practice every kind of impurity.

But that isn't what you learned about Christ. Since you have heard about Jesus and have learned the truth that comes from him, throw off your old sinful nature and your former way of life, which is corrupted by lust and deception. Instead, let the Spirit renew your thoughts and attitudes. Put on your new nature, created to be like God—truly righteous and holy."

Ephesians 4:17-24

You are a new creation in Christ, created for good works that He planned long ago. All of the limiting beliefs, obstacles and hindrances are not nearly as powerful as the Spirit of God living in you!

In this section, you are going to explore and discover your spiritual gits, talents, interests and expertise.

"There are different kinds of spiritual gifts, but the same Spirit is the source of them all. There are different kinds of service, but we serve the same Lord. God works in different ways, but it is the same God who does the work in all of us. A spiritual gift is given to each of us so we can help each other."

1 Corinthians 12:4-7

SPIRITUAL GIFTS ASSESSMENT

When you accepted Christ, you not only got saved...you were given something very special from God: a giftedness to serve God in a unique way. God's plan for your life is that you would meet a specific need in the church family, and He has gifted you in a special way to meet that need.

"As each one of us has received a gift, minister it to one another, as good stewards of the manifold grace of God."—1 Peter 4:10

If you have trusted Christ, then you have a spiritual gift! Even if you don't know what it is or don't feel particularly gifted in a specific area, the Bible teaches that you do have a special gift that you can use to serve God. And, believe it or not, your gift is vital to the work of God in our church family, otherwise God would not have placed you here.

God's Word teaches that as a member of His Body, you are important to His work in this place. He has appointed you a gift and a purpose for being here...and you will greatly enjoy discovering and using that gift for His purposes!

WHAT SHOULD YOU DO WITH THIS SPIRITUAL GIFT?

First Peter says that God wants you to be a "good steward" of His gift to you! The best way to do that is to begin now discovering, developing, and using your gift to serve the Lord and His church. The great result of using your gift is that the entire church family ministers to each other and to the community. That's the way the church, the Body of Christ, is supposed to work!

TAKING THE SPIRITUAL GIFTS ASSESSMENT

• To complete the assessment, answer every question in order by circling the number, 0 to 5, that most accurately describes yourself.

• While answering, refer to the scale indicator above the questions.

• When completing the spiritual gifts assessment, do not think as much as react.

• For the most accurate assessment answer quickly and honestly.

For best results, PRAY BEFORE ATTEMPTING.

	Never	Rarely	Occasionally	True sometimes	True most of the time	Always true
	0	1	2	3	4	5

1. I relate & measure everything I experience accordingly to God's Word.

0	1	2	3	4	5

2. Others seem to look to me for advice and help.

0	1	2	3	4	5

3. I'm easily bothered by others' lack of compassion.

0	1	2	3	4	5

4. I don't take anything at face value.

0	1	2	3	4	5

5. I can visualize the "big picture" of a major project.

0	1	2	3	4	5

6. When others are in my home I like to wait on them "hand and foot."

0	1	2	3	4	5

7. I feel compelled to give financially to others.

0	1	2	3	4	5

8. I will speak the truth whether or not it causes hurt feelings.

0	1	2	3	4	5

9. I can organize and delegate people and resources easily.

0	1	2	3	4	5

10. I feel compelled to share knowledge.

0	1	2	3	4	5

11. Discouraged people are often encouraged by my words.

0	1	2	3	4	5

12. I neglect my own work in order to help others.

0	1	2	3	4	5

13. I easily identify tasks that need to get done and do them myself.

0	1	2	3	4	5

14. I enjoy doing little things to help people.

0	1	2	3	4	5

15. My natural tendency is to step up and take control.

0	1	2	3	4	5

16. I cheerfully give time or money, regardless of how much I have to give.

0	1	2	3	4	5

17. I have compassion for all living creatures.

0	1	2	3	4	5

18. I don't hesitate to give constructive criticism.

0	1	2	3	4	5

19. People see me as a frank and outspoken person.

0	1	2	3	4	5

20. People seem to learn easily from me.

0	1	2	3	4	5

21. I can be described as responsible, charitable, and disciplined.

0	1	2	3	4	5

22. I don't expect repayment for favors I do for others.

0	1	2	3	4	5

23. Others tell me I'm a good listener.

0	1	2	3	4	5

24. Communicating the facts in a situation is something I do well.

0	1	2	3	4	5

Never	Rarely	Occasionally	True sometimes	True most of the time	Always true
0	1	2	3	4	5

25. I am a task oriented person.

    0   1   2   3   4   5

26. I find it easy to maintain an optimistic outlook.

    0   1   2   3   4   5

27. I will stand alone on something I believe in strongly.

    0   1   2   3   4   5

28. I will not confront others if I feel it may hurt them.

    0   1   2   3   4   5

29. I give well above my tithe to the Body of Christ.

    0   1   2   3   4   5

30. While I'm frugal in personal spending, I'm often led to give to others.

    0   1   2   3   4   5

31. I enjoy research as well as sharing what I find.

    0   1   2   3   4   5

32. I am compelled to comfort people who are hurting or suffering.

    0   1   2   3   4   5

33. Deadlines challenge me & I usually meet them on time.

    0   1   2   3   4   5

34. I can discern the motives of others fairly easily

    0   1   2   3   4   5

35. I find strength from bearing other's burdens.

    0   1   2   3   4   5

36. My use of knowledge may appear prideful.

    0   1   2   3   4   5

37. I can create order out of organizational chaos.

    0   1   2   3   4   5

38. I volunteer my time and talents to worthwhile causes.

    0   1   2   3   4   5

39. I'm moved with compassion to cry with others.

    0   1   2   3   4   5

40. I can select the best person for particular tasks.

    0   1   2   3   4   5

41. My focus on right and wrong may be read as being judgmental.

    0   1   2   3   4   5

42. I enjoy helping others develop a plan of action to deal with their concerns.

    0   1   2   3   4   5

Spiritual Gifts Test Scoring Key

Directions: Transfer the number you circled to the blank beside the corresponding question. Add the totals up in each column. The highest possible score in one column would be 30.

1.	6.	4.	2.	7.	5.	3.
8.	12.	10.	11.	16.	9.	17.
19.	13.	20.	18.	21.	15.	28.
27.	14.	24.	23.	22.	33.	32.
34.	25.	31.	26.	29.	37.	35.
41.	38.	36.	42.	30.	40.	39.
Totals						
Prophet/Perceiver	Server	Teacher	Exhorter/ Encourager	Giver	Leader/Administrator	Mercy/Compassion

SPIRITUAL GIFTS:

PROPHET/PERCEIVER

The God-given ability to communicate God's message in relation to the truth already revealed (Jude 3). It is not necessarily or even primarily a prediction. Rather, it is done for the purposes of encouraging, strengthening and comforting (1 Cor. 14:3). These have the ability to perceive the spiritual needs of others and meet those needs through Scripture.

CHARACTERISTICS OF A PROPHET / PERCEIVER:

1. Able to recognize good and bad and hates what is bad.
2. Sees everything clearly not dimly; no foggy or indefinite areas
3. Recognizes character in people, whether good or bad
4. Encourages repentance for the glory of God
5. Is an introvert rather than an extravert?
6. Sees the Bible as the foundation for truth
7. Courageously holds to spiritual truths
8. Outspoken
9. Powerful and persuasive speaker
10. Distraught over the sins of others
11. Sees their own shortcomings and those of others
12. Desires to see God's plans take place
13. Promotes spiritual growth in others
14. Fanatical about integrity
15. Strongly communicates what they perceive
16. Self-examiner
17. Opinionated and holds to convictions
18. Holds to a high standard
19. Desperately desires to obey God

CHALLENGES OF THE PROPHET/PERCEIVER:

1. May be judgmental and upfront
2. Delights in goal accomplishment not forward progress
3. Forcefully pushes others toward spiritual growth
4. Intolerant of other views
5. Struggles with self-image

PLACES IN THE CHURCH BODY WHERE THIS GIFT COULD BE UTILIZED:

1. Small group leader
2. Any type of lay counseling
3. Security at any church function
4. Providing oversight of any ministry function
5. Great mentors and peacemakers

SERVER

A server has the God-given ability to recognize a need and administer assistance to others. In relation to other believers, this releases them to utilize their God-given gifts (e.g. Deacons in Acts 6:1-6; 1 Corinthians 12:28; and Romans 12:7).

CHARACTERISTICS OF A SERVER:

1. Willingly meets the needs of others
2. Has a hands on approach
3. Precise and orderly
4. Detail oriented
5. Friendly
6. Has trouble turning others away
7. More interest in others than self
8. More short term orientated than long term
9. Actively expressive rather than verbally expressive
10. Desires appreciation
11. Goes above and beyond what is asked of them
12. Enjoys being helpful
13. High energy level
14. Orderly; does not like clutter
15. Perfectionist
16. Places an importance on serving
17. Would rather do than delegate
18. Supports the leadership

CHALLENGES FOR THE SERVER:

1. Criticizes those who are not serving
2. Helps others to the extent of neglecting personal family
3. So enthusiastic to help, may come across as pushy
4. Does not like to be served
5. Saddened when unappreciated

PLACES IN THE CHURCH BODY WHERE THIS GIFT COULD BE UTILIZED:

1. Hospitality ministry
2. Children's ministry
3. Homeless ministry
4. Taking meals to ill or injured
5. Set-up or tear down at special events
7. Serving anywhere, anytime, anyway
8. Construction of any type
9. Maintenance of anything
10. Putting together anything with the hands

TEACHER

The God-given ability to study, research, explain and communicate truth
(e.g. Paul andTimothy in 2 Timothy 2:2).

CHARACTERISTICS OF A TEACHER:

1. Logical presenter of truth
2. Confirms truth by examining facts
3. Enjoys study and investigation
4. Knows how to do word studies
5. Uses biblical illustrations
6. Detests Scripture used out of context
7. Establishes truth biblically
8. Objective rather than subjective
9. Extensive vocabulary
10. Accurate presenter of truth
11. Tests the information of others
12. Favors teaching over evangelism
13. Starts with Scripture when answering questions
14. Intellectual
15. Disciplined
16. Emotionally stable
17. Has a close circle of friends
18. Strong convictions based on solid research
19. Believes God's truth leads to life change

CHALLENGES FOR THE TEACHER:

1. Can neglect application in exchange for information download
2. Slow to accept views of other
3. Prideful due to knowledge
4. May be legalistic and dogmatic
5. Easily distracted by love of new interests

PLACES IN THE CHURCH BODY WHERE THIS GIFT COULD BE UTILIZED:

1. Small group leader
2. Bible study leader - Men's ministry, Women's ministry, Children's ministry
3. Rock U instructor
4. Research assistant
5. Developer of curriculum
6. Child, youth, teen mentor

EXHORTER

The God-given ability to draw near to individuals in time of need; encouraging and counseling them accurately with the Word of God; and persuading them to take courage in the face of something they must do or assuring them to take comfort because of something that has occurred (E.g. Barnabas in Acts 4:36-37; 9:26-27; 11:19-26; and 15:36-41).

CHARACTERISTICS OF A EXHORTER:

1. Verbally encouraging
2. Likes to apply the Word rather than investigate it
3. Prefers practical application over theological truth
4. Works best with others
5. Verbally encourages others to excel in ministry
6. Loves to do personal counseling
7. Loves to talk
8. Excels in communication
9. Perceives trials as opportunities for personal growth
10. Has a positive attitude
11. Easily makes decisions
12. Prefers to quickly resolve problems
13. Needs to bounce ideas off others

CHALLENGES FOR THE EXHORTER:

1. Frequently interrupts others
2. Uses Scripture out of context
3. Out spoken and opinionated
4. Slightly overconfident

PLACES IN THE CHURCH BODY WHERE THIS GIFT COULD BE UTILIZED:

1. Lay counseling
2. Stephen minister
3. Table facilitator
4. Hospitality ministry
5. Drama ministry
6. Nursing home ministry
7. Homeless Ministry Team
8. Small group leader
9. Anyplace where encouragement is needed

GIVER

The God-given ability to give freely of what God has entrusted to them. This includes giving time, material goods and financial resources with joy and eagerness and without any "ulterior motives" that would benefit the giver (E.g. David in I Chronicles 29:1-19).

CHARACTERISTICS OF A GIVER:

1. Gives as led by the Spirit
2. Freely and happily gives
3. Often gives anonymously
4. Understands giving is an intricate part of serving
5. Takes pleasure in meeting the needs of others
6. Gives not only quantity but quality
7. Gives to bless and enhance ministries
8. Sees hospitality as a chance to give
9. Financially wise
10. Strongly believes in tithes and offerings
11. Understands that God owns everything
12. Strong business skills
13. Appreciates value
14. Is not gullible

CHALLENGES FOR THE GIVER:

1. Tends to be controlling with money
2. Pressures others to be more generous
3. May over commit
4. Uses financial giving as a way out of other requirements
5. Leads others on guilt trips

PLACES IN THE CHURCH BODY WHERE THIS GIFT COULD BE UTILIZED:

1. Homeless ministry
2. Small group leader
3. Fundraising
4. Any serving opportunity
5. Hospitality ministry
6. Financial counseling ministry Team
7. Support of church special projects (i.e. building)
8. Financially support any ministry

LEADERSHIP / ADMINISTRATION

The God-given ability to lead others in meaningful endeavors which demonstrates personal care and concern in order to meet the needs of others and encourage their growth (E.g. Fathers in I Tim. 3:4-5; 12).

CHARACTERISTICS OF LEADERSHIP / ADMINISTRATION:

1. Motivates others to action
2. Clearly communicates
3. Thrives when given authority
4. Happily receives authority when given
5. Naturally assumes leadership when there is a lack
6. Takes on long-term projects
7. Is a visionary
8. Has good networking abilities
9. Delegates well
10. Takes criticism well
11. Is passionate and enthusiastic
12. Enjoys accomplishing goals
13. Gives credit to others
14. Meets challenges as they arise
15. Is a natural and capable leader
16. Understands the Big picture
17. Discards what does not work and keeps what does
18. Enjoys people
19. Dislikes the mundane routine

CHALLENGES FOR THE LEADER / ADMINISTRATOR:

1. May have trouble dealing with opposition
2. May become callous due to constant criticism
3. Pushes hard to the point of neglecting family
4. Ignores family responsibilities due to love of work

PLACES IN THE CHURCH BODY WHERE THIS GIFT COULD BE UTILIZED:

1. Small group leader
2. Jr. High ministry
3. High School ministry
4. College ministry
5. Singles ministry
6. Prison ministry
7. Any type of leadership/oversight role
8. Creator of new ministries
9. Coach of Sports ministries

MERCY / COMPASSION

The God-given ability to have immediate compassion for those who are suffering combined with great joy in meeting their needs (E.g. the Good Samaritan in Luke 10:30-37).

CHARACTERISTICS OF MERCY / COMPASSION:

1. Loves to love
2. Searches out the good in people
3. Brings out the good in people
4. Recognizes the spiritual and emotional condition of others
5. Acts out of concern for others
6. Cares for the emotional, spiritual, and physical well being of others
7. Considers others more important than self
8. Chooses words carefully
9. Recognizes the affect words can have
10. Detects insincerity
11. Loves to be thoughtful
12. Is trustworthy
13. Non-confrontational
14. Unusually cheerful
15. Thinks with the heart rather than the head
16. Rejoices and/or grieves with others

CHALLENGES FOR THE MERCY/COMPASSION:

1. Overly sensitive
2. Caring may be misunderstood by the opposite sex
3. Easily takes up others problems that are not their own
4. Thinking with their heart leads to indecision
5. Can be easily hurt by others unintentionally

PLACES IN THE CHURCH BODY WHERE THIS GIFT COULD BE UTILIZED:

1. Small group leader
2. Homeless ministry
3. Counseling ministry
4. Hospitality of any sort
5. Visitation and follow-up
6. Prison ministry
7. Greeters
8. Any type of phone work
9. Children's ministry

IMPORTANT REMINDERS

Keep in mind that oftentimes the Holy Spirit gives us more than one gift which serves to keep our other gift (gifts) in check or harmonize to create a blended gift that God uses in unique ways. This is another reason why each and everyone of us has a unique role to play in the Kingdom even if your gift may seem just like someone else you know!

1. Scripture commands us to minister in many areas whether or not we have the corresponding spiritual gift(s). For example Scripture clearly tells us that some have the following gifts, yet all are to minister in these ways…Gifts to some Commands to all

Ministering (serving) Serve one another (Galatians 5:13)

Exhortation Exhort each other (Hebrews 10:25)

Giving all give (2 Corinthians 9:7)

Teaching Make Disciples (Matthew 28:19)

Showing Mercy Be kind (Ephesians 4:32)

Faith Walk by faith (2 Corinthians 5:7)

Evangelism all witness (Acts 1:8)

Oftentimes as we are faithful to these commands, after we discover our particular spiritual gift(s).

2. No matter what spiritual gift(s) we have received, the Christian virtue of love must accompany the exercise of those gifts; otherwise, they will prove unfruitful. "If I speak with the tongues of men and of angels, but do not have love, I have become a noisy gong or a clanging cymbal. And if I have the gift of prophecy, and know all mysteries and all knowledge; and if I have all faith, so as to remove mountains, but do not have love, I am nothing. And if I give all my possessions to feed the poor, and if I deliver my body to be burned, but do not have love, it profits me nothing." 1 Corinthians 13:1-3

THE DIFFERENCE BETWEEN GIFTS AND TALENTS:
Talents have to do with techniques and methods; gifts have to do with spiritual abilities.
Talents depend on natural ability, gifts on spiritual endowment. Talents instruct, inspire, or entertain on a natural level. However, when a gift is exercised, something supernatural happens in and through the one who is ministering.

CONCLUSION:
Your God-given personality, talents, abilities and spiritual gifts all work together to make you uniquely you! "Whoever serves is to do so as one who is serving by the strength which God supplies; so that in all things God may be glorified through Jesus Christ, to whom belongs the glory and dominion forever and ever. Amen." 1 Peter 4:11

Spiritual Gifts Test used with permission from Rock Church San Diego

How exciting to discover your spiritual gifts! I think you'll find now that you aware, more opportunities to use that gift are going to open up to you.

Just as it is important to receive valid criticism so you can move forward in course correction, it's important that you understand your spiritual gifts and recognize your skills, talents, strengths and qualities.

 In this next section we will be seeking the Lord to bring to your mind and remembrance the answers to the following questions as He prepares you to set your goals.

Strengths & Qualities

List 10 qualities that you possess:
1.

2.

3.

4.

5.

6.

7.

8.

9.

10

What are the top 3 qualities that come naturally to you:

1.

2.

3.

What are the top 3 qualities you display or feel when interacting with others:

1.

2.

3.

List any positive feedback others have given you in the past:

Next you will go through a series of questions to find your sweet spot. Each graph and set of questions are the same in principal, just worded in a different way. Sometimes different ways of looking at the same thing help you see it clearer.

"We are all priests before God, there is no such distinction as 'secular or sacred.' In fact, the opposite of sacred is not secular; the opposite of sacred is profane. In short, no follower of Christ does secular work. We all have a sacred calling." Ravi Zacharias

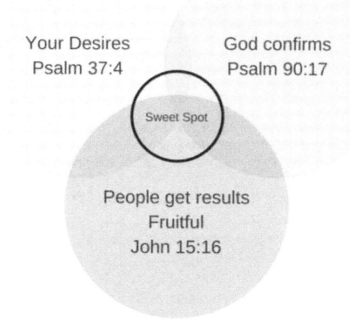

Your Desires
Psalm 37:4

God confirms
Psalm 90:17

Sweet Spot

People get results
Fruitful
John 15:16

1. *"Delight yourself also in the* LORD, *And He shall give you the desires of your heart." Psalm 37:4*

   What is the desire the Lord is putting in your heart?

1. *"Let the favor of the Lord our God be upon us; And confirm for us the work of our hands; Yes, confirm the work of our hands." Psalm 90:17*

   Do you perceive the Lord confirming this work to you? Perhaps in your spirit or through others?

2. *"You did not choose me, but I chose you and appointed you so that you might go and bear fruit—fruit that will last—and so that whatever you ask in my name the Father will give you." John 15:16*

   From what activities do you see fruit coming from?

Small disclaimer when it comes to question 3 and whether you see people getting results. Don't bank all your plans on that question. You may not see results or fruit in your lifetime. That doesn't mean you aren't in God's perfect will.

Jeremiah was known as the weeping prophet. In his entire ministry people gave little weight to his message of repentance. Listen to his complaint, *"Then I said, "What sorrow is mine, my mother. Oh, that I had died at birth! I am hated everywhere I go. I am neither a lender who threatens to foreclose nor a borrower who refuses to pay— yet they all curse me."* Jeremiah 15:10*

Ezekiel too had a hard calling. Listen to what God tells Ezekiel, *"Son of man,"* he said, *"I am sending you to the nation of Israel, a rebellious nation that has rebelled against me. They and their ancestors have been rebelling against me to this very day. They are a stubborn and hard-hearted people. But I am sending you to say to them, 'This is what the Sovereign LORD says!' And whether they listen or refuse to listen—for remember, they are rebels—at least they will know they have had a prophet among them.*

"Son of man, do not fear them or their words. Don't be afraid even though their threats surround you like nettles and briers and stinging scorpions. Do not be dismayed by their dark scowls, even though they are rebels. You must give them my messages whether they listen or not. But they won't listen, for they are completely rebellious!

Sometimes when you do what God calls you to do, the only one who is pleased is God Himself. Pleased by your obedience. This is a good time to practice just living for an audience of One.

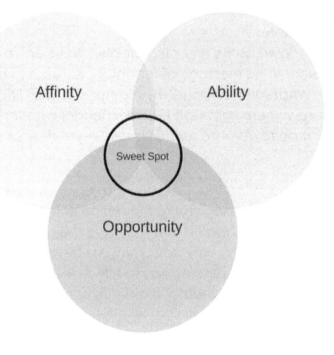

1. What do you have an affinity (natural liking) for?

2. Do you also the ability that goes with it?

3. Do you have the opportunity to do it?

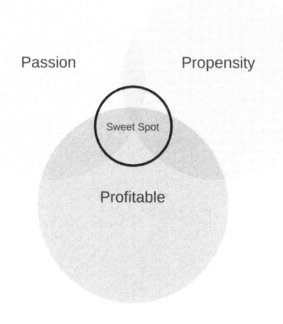

1. What are you passionate about?

2. Do you have a natural inclination or talent that goes with it?

3. Will it be profitable in some way?

"God made me fast. And when I run, I feel His pleasure."
Eric Liddell

CHAPTER 6

REFLECTION

Last Year's Recap

1. What was the smartest thing you did in the past 12 months?

2. What 3 things happened you never want to happen again?

3. What are 3 things that went really well?

4. List 3 things you feel you could have done better:

5. Choose 1 act of service you did that helped another person, glorified God and blessed you:

Success Recap

1.   Write down an area that you have had or are having success in.

2.   What are/were you doing to have that success?

3.   What unique talents, ideas, strengths or life experiences helped you accomplish that success?

4.   What about it made you feel alive, positive and effective?

5.   What specific things can you replicate to help you succeed in your current goals?

Not To-Do List

If you are like me you keep a To-Do list. Writing down what I need to do keeps me on track. This year I also started a "Not To-Do" list that keeps me on track as well. Different from a goal, these are habits that will hinder me and need to be changed. Here are some of the current things on my list.

NOT TO-DO

1. Say yes without praying first.
2. Scroll social media while lying in bed.
3. Eat inflammatory foods.
4. Procrastinate tasks that bore me.

What comes to mind that should be added to your Not To-Do list:

1.

2.

3.

4.

5.

6.

7.

8.

"The fastest way to success is to replace bad habits with good habits." Zig Ziglar

Habits to put in place for success:

Here are some of mine:

1. Pause and be ready to say, "I will get back with you" when someone asks for something.
2. Read books before I go to sleep.
3. Meal plan and prep *consistently*.
4. Eat more vegetables.
5. Get more sleep.
6. Live every day like I'm going on vacation tomorrow.

What habits do you need to put into place that will help you accomplish your NOT-To-Do list and become more productive so you can achieve your goals?

1. Live every day like I'm going on vacation tomorrow.

2.

3.

4.

5.

6.

7.

8.

I took the liberty of adding number 1 to your list. This one mindset/habit has made me more productive than anything else.

Think about the last time you went on vacation. You probably cleared everything on your desk, responded to emails, scheduled meetings and handled anything that was pending. If you have a quota to meet you probably hustled to get it done. You most likely cleaned your house, changed your sheets and did away with any clutter leaving it tidy and clean for your house sitter. That is how we should live every day. It may not be realistic (especially if doing all that required you to live on 4 hours of sleep) but if you can make that your standard and keep it a good majority of the time, just imagine how your life would change. Raise your standards!

With that productive attitude in mind, we can't be all work and no play. God wants us to rest and recharge and enjoy the good things He has given us for our pleasure. Whether you tend toward being a workaholic or not, it's important to add pleasurable activities to our goals and schedules as well. Take some time to reflect on the things that you enjoy and list 10 of them here:

1.

2.

3.

4.

5.

6.

7.

8.

9.

10.

Failure

Failure is a tough pill to swallow. But we make a grave mistake if we run from it. In trying to bury it and quickly move on we can lose the lesson that may just hold the key to our success. God's conviction is heathy and life giving. Satan's condemnation is full of death and despair. Failure can be looked at through either lens.

As Believers we should know that it is God's kindness that leads us to repentance. (Romans 2:4) Sometimes that kindness is Him allowing us to feel sorrow for our sin. (2 Corinthians 7:10) As God's kindness leads us to repentance, it is clear that it is leaves us with no regret as we turn away from the wrong way to the right way. Whether we are talking about salvation and sin or talking about not accomplishing goals, there is now no condemnation to those who are in Christ. We can and should look at our failures with brutal honesty with no shame and no discouragement knowing God is for us!

Victory Over Failures

List any goals you had this past year or quarter that you didn't accomplish:

5 Why's

I love this exercise. I do this quite often when I am praying and journaling and am always surprised by how quickly God answers me and helps me identify at least 5 reasons why I did or didn't do something.

Column 1- Ask God why you didn't achieve this (or these) goals.
List the 5 why's in the first column of the table below. They will either fall under external reasons or thoughts and limiting beliefs. (There is enough room for 10 reasons.)

Column 2- Ask God what the solution is. For external reasons, be practical. For thoughts and limiting beliefs use scripture and yield that Sword of the Spirit.

External Example Maybe your goal was to join a get a personal trainer a couple of times a month to supplement your workout but you didn't accomplish that because you didn't have the money. A possible **external** solution in Column 2 could be to stop getting Starbucks every day and instead drink coffee at home.

Internal Thought or Limiting Belief Example Maybe you didn't accomplish the goal of getting involved in a small group at church. If your reason was that you were afraid of being vulnerable in a group and asking for help, then you would want to use a verse of scripture that combats that **internal** fear/lie.

We call those put-offs and put-ons. You put off the old sin nature, your flesh which is influenced by Satan and instead put on the new nature which is directed by the Spirit of God living in you.

In this case of fear, you could quote and meditate on *2 Timothy 1:7 "For God has not given us a spirit of fear, but of power and of love and of a sound mind."*

Column 1- Put-Off's	Column 2- Put-On's
Why happened externally that caused you to not complete these? 1. 2. 3. 4. 5. What internal thoughts or limiting beliefs did you have that caused you to not complete these? 1. 2. 3. 4. 5.	What external things should you do instead that will lead to success? 1. 2. 3. 4. 5. Using your scripture or promises of God, what should you be thinking instead? 1. 2. 3. 4. 5.

Do you need more time, money, accountability or faith to achieve these? Write down which and some ways you can get that.

Based on what you've discovered, journal about what you will do differently in the future to accomplish your goals:

Imagine it is one year from now....

Write out all the things you have accomplished. Keep in mind what you will regret if you don't do and what matters most to you this year.

An Anchor for Your Soul

This past year I was desperate to not have another replay of the previous year. I sat with the Lord and asked for a fresh guiding word, phrase, and verse to apply to my year.

Word: My anchor word was **discipline**. All of my goals were going to require me to be disciplined. There were lots of descriptive words that applied, but discipline was the one that really resonated with me.

Phrase: After having been in quite a challenging season with health issues, financial pressures, strain on my marriage and most tragically the death of my brother I was battling anticipatory fear. I found myself continually waiting for the other shoe to drop. It really became an automatic reaction that something bad was just around the corner. It was in prayer that I realized I was living that way. Hopeful expectancy was something I was desperately missing! So "Hopeful Expectancy" became my phrase for the year.

Verse: Then I chose a verse that I had never memorized or quoted before. If there was one thing I was relearning and experiencing again it was that I am completely dependent on the Lord and His favor on my life. Psalm 44:3 jumped off the page to me, "*For they did not gain possession of the land by their own sword, nor did their own arm save them; but it was Your right hand, Your arm, and the light of Your countenance, because You favored them.*"

Prayerfully seek God for an anchor to hold on to. What word, what phrase, and what verse will be your guide or anchor?

Word:

Phrase:

Verse:

CHAPTER 7

GOAL SETTING

In **God's Way to Success** we will be looking at all the areas of our life: occupational, spiritual, physical, emotional, relational as we set goals in these areas- all under the umbrella of God's purpose and plan.

Annual Goals

God Sized Smart Goals	Categories to consider:
<ul><li>**S**pecific</li><li>**M**easurable</li><li>**A**bove what you can achieve on your own (God Size)</li><li>**R**elevant</li><li>**T**imely</li></ul>	<ul><li>Physical</li><li>Spiritual</li><li>Financial</li><li>Professional</li><li>Personal Growth</li><li>Environment- home, office, vehicle</li><li>Relationships Family/Friends</li><li>Purpose/Calling</li></ul>

While I don't want you to overwhelm yourself with too many goals, you are body, soul (mind, will, emotions) and spirit and will need to consider prayerfully what to focus on. Ask God to lead you into the goals and the areas of life He is working on. I am giving you worksheets for 10 goals, but please only do as many God is giving you.

"Now glory be to God, who by His mighty power at work within us is able to do far more than we would ever dare to ask or even dream of—infinitely beyond our highest prayers, desires, thoughts, or hopes."
Ephesians 3:20

Explanations and instructions for using the goal setting sheets

Category (i.e.: Spiritual, Physical, Financial etc.) _____

Write the goal:
Make it as specific and measurable as possible. Don't limit yourself because God is able to do the impossible. (However, if you can't sing then it would be a deceptive goal and off of God's course for your life to win a grammy!) Make it relevant and timely to your gifts, talents, expertise, experience.

Scripture: Is there a verse of scripture that goes with this? Google it or use a concordance searching for a key word. Write out the verse.

Will this glorify God? Is it in line with the character and expressed will of God. If it violates scripture then you can be certain it won't glorify Him.

Will this bless others? Who?
Think of who will benefit from your obedience.

WHY- What is your why? Write at least 3 reasons you want/need to achieve this goal.

Action Steps to Take:
Your Part: Obey (things that are in your control and you need to obey God in) Here are a couple examples of your part. If you are writing a book, then obey by sitting down and writing every day for an hour. Obey by praying and seeking God.

A farmer obeys and plows the field, prepares the soil, sows the seed, waters the seed.

God's Part: Trust (things that need to happen but are out of your control. You must trust God for these things.) Here are just a couple examples of God's part. You have to trust God to give you the time and inspiration. Trust God to influence people to buy the book.

Trust that it is God who grows the crop.

"I planted the seed in your hearts, and Apollos watered it, but it was God who made it grow." 1 Corinthians 3:6

EXAMPLE of Trust & Obey
In the story of David and Goliath we see an example of David taking action and doing his own part (obey) while depending on God (trust)to do what only God can do.

*"Then David said to the Philistine, "You come to me with a sword and with a spear and with a javelin, but **I come to you** in the name of the LORD of hosts, the God of the armies of Israel, whom you have defied. This day **the LORD will deliver you** into my hand, and **I will strike you** down and cut off your head. And **I will give** the dead bodies of the host of the Philistines this day to the birds of the air and to the wild beasts of the earth, that all the earth may know that there is a God in Israel, 47 and that all this assembly may know that the LORD saves not with sword and spear. For the battle is the LORD's, and **he will give you** into our hand." 1 Samuel 17:45-47*

Many times, we get stuck on the unknowns so we don't move forward with our dreams and goals. We just can't figure out how a certain thing will happen so we stop. Discerning between your part and God's part takes the pressure off. Just logically do what you can and leave it to God to do what only He can do.

Obey God in your part and trust Him for His part.

"From that time on your decisions should be based on whatever seems best under the circumstances, for the Lord will guide you." 1 Samuel 10:7

Accountability: What is your plan to stay accountable?
I have achieved goals with accountability and without it. A good rule of thumb for me is if I keep setting the goal and not achieving it, then I know it is time to bring someone alongside me! It could be a life coach, a personal trainer, a group fitness class, a friend, a peer, a pastor, a mentor. Any expert who you trust to encourage and keep you accountable.

Category _____

Write the goal:

Scripture: Is there a verse of scripture that goes with this?

Will this glorify God?   **Will this bless others?**   **Who?**

WHY- What is your why? Write at least 3 reasons you want/need to achieve this goal:

Action Steps to Take:
Your Part OBEY (things that are in your control)

God's Part TRUST (things that need to happen but are out of your control)

Accountability: What is your plan to stay accountable?

What will your life look like when you accomplish this goal?

Category _____

Write the goal:

Scripture: Is there a verse of scripture that goes with this?

Will this glorify God?   **Will this bless others?**   **Who?**

WHY- What is your why? Write at least 3 reasons you want/need to achieve this goal:

Action Steps to Take:
Your Part OBEY (things that are in your control)

God's Part TRUST (things that need to happen but are out of your control)

Accountability: What is your plan to stay accountable?

What will your life look like when you accomplish this goal?

Category _____

Write the goal:

Scripture: Is there a verse of scripture that goes with this?

Will this glorify God?   **Will this bless others?**   **Who?**

WHY- What is your why? Write at least 3 reasons you want/need to achieve this goal:

Action Steps to Take:
Your Part OBEY (things that are in your control)

God's Part TRUST (things that need to happen but are out of your control)

Accountability: What is your plan to stay accountable?

What will your life look like when you accomplish this goal?

Category _____

Write the goal:

Scripture: Is there a verse of scripture that goes with this?

Will this glorify God?   **Will this bless others?**   **Who?**

WHY- What is your why? Write at least 3 reasons you want/need to achieve this goal:

Action Steps to Take:
Your Part OBEY (things that are in your control)

God's Part TRUST (things that need to happen but are out of your control)

Accountability: What is your plan to stay accountable?

What will your life look like when you accomplish this goal?

Category _____

Write the goal:

Scripture: Is there a verse of scripture that goes with this?

Will this glorify God?   **Will this bless others?**   **Who?**

WHY- What is your why? Write at least 3 reasons you want/need to achieve this goal:

Action Steps to Take:
Your Part OBEY (things that are in your control)

God's Part TRUST (things that need to happen but are out of your control)

Accountability: What is your plan to stay accountable?

What will your life look like when you accomplish this goal?

Category _____

Write the goal:

Scripture: Is there a verse of scripture that goes with this?

Will this glorify God?   **Will this bless others?**   **Who?**

WHY- What is your why? Write at least 3 reasons you want/need to achieve this goal:

Action Steps to Take:
Your Part OBEY (things that are in your control)

God's Part TRUST (things that need to happen but are out of your control)

Accountability: What is your plan to stay accountable?

What will your life look like when you accomplish this goal?

Category _____

Write the goal:

Scripture: Is there a verse of scripture that goes with this?

Will this glorify God?   **Will this bless others?**   **Who?**

WHY- What is your why? Write at least 3 reasons you want/need to achieve this goal:

Action Steps to Take:
Your Part OBEY (things that are in your control)

God's Part TRUST (things that need to happen but are out of your control)

Accountability: What is your plan to stay accountable?

What will your life look like when you accomplish this goal?

Category _____

Write the goal:

Scripture: Is there a verse of scripture that goes with this?

Will this glorify God?   **Will this bless others?**   **Who?**

WHY- What is your why? Write at least 3 reasons you want/need to achieve this goal:

Action Steps to Take:
Your Part OBEY (things that are in your control)

God's Part TRUST (things that need to happen but are out of your control)

Accountability: What is your plan to stay accountable?

What will your life look like when you accomplish this goal?

Category _____

Write the goal:

Scripture: Is there a verse of scripture that goes with this?

Will this glorify God?   **Will this bless others?**   **Who?**

WHY- What is your why? Write at least 3 reasons you want/need to achieve this goal:

Action Steps to Take:
Your Part OBEY (things that are in your control)

God's Part TRUST (things that need to happen but are out of your control)

Accountability: What is your plan to stay accountable?

What will your life look like when you accomplish this goal?

Category _____

Write the goal:

Scripture: Is there a verse of scripture that goes with this?

Will this glorify God?   **Will this bless others?**   **Who?**

WHY- What is your why? Write at least 3 reasons you want/need to achieve this goal:

Action Steps to Take:
Your Part OBEY (things that are in your control)

God's Part TRUST (things that need to happen but are out of your control)

Accountability: What is your plan to stay accountable?

What will your life look like when you accomplish this goal?

CHAPTER 8

KEYS TO SUCCESS

Keys to Success

Daily Routine

John C. Maxwell said "The secret of your success lies in your daily routine." We've already touched on your rhythm, but I want you to really clarify what are your absolute musts in a daily routine that will make for the most fruitful day and set you up for success.

Prayer

When you study the gospels, we see Jesus continually going out alone to spend time with His Father in prayer. The disciples who witnessed the miracles of Jesus became mighty prayer warriors and saw their own miracles. In both Matthew and Luke we read that they specifically asked Jesus to teach them to pray. It's probably safe to say that they understood there was a direct connection between the miracles, the love and the power, and the time that Jesus spent alone in prayer.

How different would your life look if you spent time in prayer every day? Matthew 6:6 says, *"But you, when you pray, go into your inner room, close your door and pray to your Father who is in secret, and your Father who sees what is done in secret will reward you."* If you've heard my testimony about the Lord delivering me from a meth addiction, one of the things I talk about is how the day before I got clean it looked to all outside appearances like any other day of my addiction. Actually, it looked and felt that way to me as well. But unbeknownst to most people I had been seeking God with all my heart and praying fervently to Him. What was done in secret was openly rewarded.

Business success, weight loss, harmonious relationships, whatever your goal may be, if it is God's will and you are praying for it, you can be assured you will have what you've asked. 1 John 5:14-15 says, *"And we are confident that he hears us whenever we ask for anything that pleases him. And since we know he hears us when we make our requests, we also know that he will give us what we ask for."*

Prayer is also much more than us talking and asking, it is also us listening and perceiving what God is saying to us through His word and very personally and specifically through the guidance of the Holy Spirit. We should know that God will never give us a goal that violates His Word. A good example of this would be if we are struggling with money, it would never be His will that we steal or do something unethical to get money. That is pretty black and white. But what about gray areas that are not specifically addressed in His word? Gray areas like, what job do you take, what do you drop off your schedule, what ministry should you serve in, etc. You can be assured when you are walking by faith that if you indeed have sought the Lord even though you may be a little unsure, He is directing your steps. *"Trust in the Lord with all your heart, and lean not on your own understanding; in all your ways acknowledge Him, and He shall direct your paths." Proverbs 3:5–6*

"Do not be conformed to this world, but be transformed by the renewal of your mind, that by testing you may discern what is the will of God, what is good and acceptable and perfect." Romans 12:2

During prayer ask the Lord to reveal to you the things that are weighing you down from running the race He has set before you or the sins that are hindering you. (Hebrews 12:1) Talk to God about your goals. Keep a loose grip so He can take away what is simply good and give you what is best. Listen to His promptings and be prepared to leave your prayer closet and take steps of faith. It'll please Him and bless you!

"...The earnest prayer of a righteous person has great power and produces wonderful results." James 5:16

"Call to Me, and I will answer you, and show you great and mighty things, which you do not know." Jeremiah 33:3

Lastly and most important, prayer is where we get to know God. It is in experiencing Him for who He is and having a close intimate relationship with Him that we find true fulfillment and our purpose. Yes, we need things. Yes, He invites us to make requests but ultimately if have Him, we have all we really need. So, remember to seek His face and not just His hand.

"When You said, "Seek My face," my heart said to You,
"Your face, O LORD, I shall seek." Psalm 27:8

With all the promises of prayer and because it is part of the whole armor of God, it's no surprise Satan tries to keep us from it. It foils his plans. Don't let him distract or discourage you. Make prayer a part of your daily routine.

The Word of God

His Word is alive and active. His Word never returns void but will accomplish what He sends it out for. He told Joshua if he wanted success then he should meditate on the Word of God day and night. His Word is full of His faithful promises to His children. His Word reveals to us who He is and what He can do. It reveals to us who we are now if we've been born again and trusted in Christ as our Lord and Savior. It reveals to us the power and authority that comes with our new identity as beloved children of God. His Word is the bread of life. Our bibles, written by God Himself through the pens of inspired men are the most precious and powerful books ever written. He will use it to change your life and bring you into your calling. Right beliefs lead to right living.

As part of your daily routine, reading your bible will transform you from the inside out. As transformation happens deep inside you your behavior on the outside will adapt and change as well. When you have good soil of the heart and the Word of God gets planted in it, you will have a crop of 30, 60 even 100 times more than was sown!

"So then faith comes by hearing, and hearing by the word of God."
Romans 10:17

When your faith builds through hearing God's Word it will be easier and easier for you to walk by faith outside of your comfort zone instead of letting your feelings lead you. What a great way to tackle the day and be a doer! Plus, having faith brings you a confident joy and peace when you can't yet see what you are trusting God for. That is exactly what you need on a daily basis as you work on your goals.

"What is faith? It is the confident assurance that something we want is going to happen. It is the certainty that what we hope for is waiting for us, even though we cannot see it up ahead."
Hebrews 11:1

- Jesus looked at them and said, "With man this is impossible, but with God all things are possible." Matthew 19:26

- "I am the LORD, the God of all mankind. Is anything too hard for me?" Jeremiah 32:27

Praise and Worship

I start each day with thanking God before I even get out of bed. I thank Him for a brand-new day, for all He has planned for me, that His tender mercies and compassions are brand new and then I quote *Psalm 118:24,* *"This is the day the LORD has made; We will rejoice and be glad in it."* I don't do it mindlessly like some kind of ritual with no meaning, I truly do it from a heart of gratitude and to begin to think truth. It's the foundation of my day. While I get my coffee, I choose one of my favorite worship songs and start my morning singing to the Lord. *(Some of my favorites for the morning are Morning Has Broken by Third Day, Give Me Jesus by Jeremy Camp, 10,000 Reasons by Matt Redman.)* I don't necessarily like getting out of bed, but once I am up I'm on, so I enjoy music first thing. I realize some people prefer quiet so my routine may not be appealing to you!

Jesus is so worthy of praise and worship. You and I were not purchased with corruptible gold or silver, but with the precious blood of Jesus Christ. His personal love and commitment to us is unmatchable. We should continue to be amazed by that. For those of us who love Him and are called according to His purpose there is nothing that will happen that won't work out for good for us. (Romans 8:28) That fact should produce thanksgiving, praise and worship!

Mindset & Meditation

Waiting Patiently & Expectantly

There are those days though that I am overwhelmed, discouraged, confused and can feel fear of failure or just anticipatory fear come over me as I seek to do what I believe God is calling me to. Usually it is because I have taken my eyes off the Lord because of some circumstance or am allowing myself to grow weary in waiting. Daily I hold onto His promises but on days like that I hold on to and mediate on some very specific verses that speak to the waiting.

- "But they who wait for the Lord shall renew their strength; they shall mount up with wings like eagles; they shall run and not be weary; they shall walk and not faint." Isaiah 40:31

- "That is why I wait expectantly, trusting God to help, for he has promised." Psalm 130:5

- "I waited patiently for the LORD to help me, and he turned to me and heard my cry." Psalm 40:1

- "For promotion and power come from nowhere on earth, but only from God. He promotes one and deposes another." Psalm 75:6-7

- "So let's not get tired of doing what is good. At just the right time we will reap a harvest of blessing if we don't give up." Galatians 6:9

- "Be anxious for nothing, but in everything by prayer and supplication, with thanksgiving, let your requests be made known to God and the peace of God, which surpasses all understanding, will guard your hearts and minds through Christ Jesus. Philippians 4:6-7

- Finally, brethren, whatever things are true, whatever things are noble, whatever things are just, whatever things are pure, whatever things are lovely, whatever things are of good report, if there is any virtue and if there

is anything praiseworthy—meditate on these things."
Philippians 4:8

Focus on your what and why when you don't know the how and when.

Part of the daily mindset in regards to goals should be on **WHAT** the goal is (keeping it top of mind) and on the **WHY**, so that when the going gets tough you have a compelling reason to push through.

The HOW should be covered in your action steps discerning what part is yours and what part is God's. But even when you know your part, sometimes you can still struggle with doubts because you just can't imagine HOW God will do His part!

Here is an anchor for your soul and mine when that comes up: *"Your road led through the sea, your pathway through the mighty waters—a pathway no one knew was there!" Psalm 77:19*

God has ways you don't know about. So, relax.

And what about the WHEN? When God when? *"He has made everything beautiful in its time." Ecclesiastes 3:11*

Work Hard by God's Grace

"But whatever I am now, it is all because God poured out his special favor on me—and not without results. For I have worked harder than any of the other apostles; yet it was not I but God who was working through me by his grace." 1 Corinthians 15:10

God gives us what we need to succeed at what He is calling us to. The wisest man who ever lived, King Solomon is responsible for much of the book of Proverbs. He requested wisdom of God to lead His people. You a child of God now have the same wisdom that you can pull from for success. Rather than comment on these verses I just want to share them with you and ask you to ponder each one, jotting down anything that comes to mind and take it directly to God in prayer. What is He revealing to you?

- Hard work means prosperity; only a fool idles away his time. Proverbs 12:11

- …hard work returns many blessings to him. Proverbs 12:14

- Work hard and become a leader; be lazy and never succeed. Proverbs 12:24

- The lazy man does not roast what he took in hunting, but diligence is man's precious possession. Proverbs 12: 27

- Any enterprise is built by wise planning, becomes strong through common sense, and profits wonderfully by keeping abreast of the facts. Proverbs 24:3-4

- Good planning and hard work lead to prosperity, but hasty shortcuts lead to poverty. Proverbs 21:5

- In all toil there is profit, but mere talk tends only to poverty. Proverbs 14:23

- We can make our plans, but the final outcome is in God's hands. Proverbs 16:1

- Commit your actions to the LORD, and your plans will succeed. Proverbs 16:3

- We should make plans—counting on God to direct us. Proverbs 16:9

- God blesses those who obey him; happy the man who puts his trust in the Lord. Proverbs 16:20

"And God is able to make all grace abound toward you, that you, always having all sufficiency in all things, may have an abundance for every good work." 2 Corinthians 9:8

"Improvise, Adapt and Overcome." -The Marines

Rest & Recover

The bible is not a buffet where we pick and choose what we like and ignore the rest. We need to look at the full counsel of God's Word. We just saw in our daily routines we should work hard but now we are going to look at resting and recovering.

In the beginning of creation, we see God resting on the seventh day.

We are told in scripture to keep the Sabbath holy (set apart).

Israel was instructed to let the land rest every 7 years.

It's clearly important to God that we rest be incorporated into our lives. He wants us to have periods of quiet, of rest, of recovery.

Once a week we should cease from our work and do what recharges us. Everyday is the Lord's Day so worshipping and being in relationship with God isn't just reserved for Sunday's. In addition, we can now enter in to the rest of God because of what Christ has done for us on the cross. We no longer need to work for our salvation. We receive it by grace through faith. (Ephesians 2:8-10).

I do make sure that I have one day a week to stop working and recharge. That is one day I do not cross my boundaries. I schedule absolutely nothing so I can have one day where I am able to do whatever I want to do. It is a rare thing to see me go workout or go to any event or get together on a Sunday. I much prefer to get alone in nature or do things around my house. It's also considered family day so my husband and I reserve that day strictly for us.

"It is useless for you to work so hard from early morning until late at night, anxiously working for food to eat; for God gives rest to his loved ones." Psalm 127:2

Not only does rest or lack of affect us spiritually but also physically. Cutting back on sleep to get more done will only backfire in the end.

As part of our daily routine you should make getting enough good quality sleep a priority. Secular studies prove why God wants His beloved to get sleep.

- The National Sleep Foundation says we're 12 percent more likely to die prematurely if we don't get the recommended seven to nine hours a night.
- Various studies show that getting less than the recommended seven to nine hours of sleep are linked to:
    - Lack of concentration
    - Memory issues
    - Diabetes
    - Heart disease
    - Inflammation
    - Mood changes
    - Accidents
    - Weakened immunity

It is during the rest period of sleeping after exercise that the muscles rebuild and you become stronger. In this we can see that rest is just as important as working hard.

Back to God's instruction to let the land rest, if the land doesn't, it loses the minerals -which is why our food lacks the nutrients it once had. How much more will our bodies deteriorate quicker when pushed to limits that God never intended.

For some of us we desire to keep going and going! Others struggle with being slothful and not going when they should. Either way we need to be wise!

I shared with you earlier that I had been diagnosed with fibromyalgia. Part of my recovery was slowing down and getting more rest. Treating my body like the temple of God that it is included proper diet and nutrition, supplements, stress management, soaking in hot baths every night, fresh air, sunshine, quiet time, and plenty of water and sleep. Essentially my body had crashed and it took time and effort and the grace of God to recover. He led me every step of the way to get to the root of my health issues. It was in implementing God's principals that I found my healing.

"He makes me lie down in green pastures; He leads me beside quiet waters. He restores my soul; He guides me in the paths of righteousness For His name's sake." Psalm 23:2-3

'Not by might, nor by power, but by my Spirit, says the Lord Almighty—you will succeed because of my Spirit, though you are few and weak.' Zechariah 4:6

Not every illness can be healed by doing the things I did. But implementing healthy practices which are wise will definitely have an impact on how you feel.

We must remember we are body, soul and spirit. Make it a part of your daily routine to attend with loving care to your whole health by drawing near to God and seeking closeness with Him, loving Him and loving others and treating your body as the temple of the Holy Spirit.

If you want to accomplish the goals that God has set before choose life and do the wise things at each crossroad. Small things done with consistency produce great results.

Be intentional about your daily routine. Be intentional about choosing life.

"Today I have given you the choice between life and death, between blessings and curses. Now I call on heaven and earth to witness the choice you make. Oh, that you would choose life, so that you and your descendants might live! You can make this choice by loving the LORD your God, obeying him, and committing yourself firmly to him. This is the key to your life."
Deuteronomy 30:19-20

CHAPTER 9

SUCCESS PLANNING

"But be doers of the word, and not hearers only, deceiving yourselves." James 1:22

Active faith takes action. As a believer if I were to ask you if you believed the promises of scripture about who God is, what He can do and who He says you are and what you can do, I am certain you would say yes, you believe. Now it is time to for those beliefs to go from passive to active. The whole purpose of you going deep in your beliefs and in scripture before setting your goals was to get you to a point where you have a solid foundation for taking action knowing that God is for you and directing you to "take the land". As you make your plans I want you to do it with your eyes on Jesus. I also aim to take the fear or emotion out of it by you writing it down. Once you've got it written down just plan on doing it. No more analyzing or chickening out! Remember you are responsible for your part and God for His part and His timing. He knows the full plan.

"I will not do it all in one year, for the land would become a wilderness, and the wild animals would become too many to control. But I will drive them out a little at a time, until your population has increased enough to fill the land. And I will set your enlarged boundaries from the Red Sea to the Philistine coast, and from the southern deserts as far as the Euphrates River; and I will cause you to defeat the people now living in the land, and you will drive them out ahead of you." Exodus 23:29-31

Your Planner

In this planner you will find:

- 1 page for your annual goals
- 1 sample daily page for each quarter
- 12 monthly task list pages
- 4 quarterly goal pages
- 4 quarterly recap pages

Today is the day! God's Way to Success has been intentionally designed that you can start it at any time. Today is always the first day of the rest of your life so you DO NOT have to wait until the beginning of a new year to set annual goals. Just pick up wherever you are and set your annual goals, then jump in the planner to whatever quarter it is.

Smart Phone I do have a smart phone and I use it to schedule my client appointments, but that is all I use it for. I keep my plans and action steps in my journal/notebook planner which is set up just like the pages you'll find. I encourage you to handwrite your action steps and goals down on paper not just on your phone. I have included a sample of the Daily Page that I use. You can make copies of it or incorporate the format into your own notebook or planner.

Why use paper and pen?

Neuroscience studies have shown that the act of handwriting your goals rather than typing them significantly increases neural pathways. And writing your goals in general whether typed or handwritten significantly increases your odds of achieving them. There was a reason God told us to write them down.

"Write the vision and make *it* plain on tablets, that he may run who reads it. For the vision *is* yet for an appointed time; But at the end it will speak, and it will not lie. Though it tarries, wait for it; Because it will surely come, It will not tarry." Habakkuk 2:2-3

Next Steps:

Quarterly:
- List your goals and keep them in front of you.
- Do a quarterly recap.
- If you are a visual learner or just creative, find pictures or words from magazines that represent your goals and create a vision board so you're reminded of your what and why.

Monthly:
- Create task list.
- Review previous months task list. Transfer any undone tasks over.
- Do your 5 whys if you didn't accomplish, then recalibrate.

Weekly:
- Review progress and add action steps to planner.
- If you are doing accountability, keep in touch with partner/group/coach via email, phone or in person.

Daily:
- Read and pray over it DAILY. Keep it Top of Mind.
- Do action step(s).

Accountability

The American Society of Training and Development (ASTD) did a study on completing goals and found the following statistics:
The probability of completing a goal if:
- You have an idea or a goal: 10%
- You consciously decide you will do it: 25%
- You decide when you will do it: 40%
- You plan how you will do it: 50%
- You commit to someone you will do it: 65%
- You have a specific accountability appointment with a person you've committed to: **95%**

If you are continually struggling to accomplish a task or a goal, maybe it's time to ask for help.

"Plans fail for lack of counsel, but with many advisers they succeed." Proverbs 15:22

"Our greatest fear should not be of failure, but of succeeding at something that doesn't really matter." Dwight L. Moody

How to use the Pages

Annual Goal Page

Using the worksheets, write out all the goals you set here. This is what you'll look at every day. I suggest you take it out of the book or make a copy of it so it's easily accessible.

I keep mine on a bulletin board that I see every day. It is also what I use to pray for my goals on a daily basis.

Quarterly Goal Page

I use this the same as I use the annual goal page. The only difference is many times it gets more specific as the year goes on or if I've accomplished a goal already, I take it off the list.

Quarterly Recap

Assess what went well and what didn't so you can recalibrate.

Monthly Task List

Every month I make a task list of everything that needs to be that month to keep on track with my quarterly or annual goals. I go to my full worksheets that have the goals and the action steps and I write down what action steps I need to take that month.

Daily Planner Pages

I typically fill in my planner for the week on Sunday nights or first thing Monday morning.

Schedule: I fill in my meetings and appointments first so I know when I will have time at my desk to work on the tasks.

To-Do: I refer back to the monthly task list and add tasks. I also add any tasks that have come up that need to be attended to.

Outfits & Menu Sections:

To make my crazy busy weeks a little smoother I like to determine what I will wear when I fill in my planner for the week. I look at the week, the weather forecast, where I am going and what I have to do. I know it sounds a little obsessive but the less decisions I have to make in the moment the more I can stay on track. Before I go to bed I simply have to put out the clothes I have already decided on for the day. When I worked outside of the house and had to pack for my workout and then something casual and comfortable after work this made my life a whole lot easier.

I also figure out what is for dinner all week long and pencil that in. Determining what I'll eat helps me with two very important things- grocery shopping and staying on track with eating. Both of those advance my goals.

Last Thoughts

Remember as you seek God's face and set out to accomplish your goals to enjoy each day. Don't wait until you reach each goal to be happy. Life is truly about the journey.

> May the LORD bless you
> and protect you.
> May the LORD smile on you
> and be gracious to you.
> May the LORD show you his favor
> and give you his peace.
> Numbers 6:24-26

ANNUAL GOALS

1ST QUARTER GOALS

Today's Plan

Day of the Week: **Date:**

To Do:

Schedule:

Dinner:

Notes:

Outfit:

Monthly Tasks- Month of:

Monthly Tasks- Month of:

Monthly Tasks- Month of:

Quarterly Recap

- What was the smartest thing you did this quarter?

- What 3 things happened you never want to happen again?

- What are 3 things that went really well?

- List 3 things you feel you could have done better:

- Pick 1 act of service you did that helped another person, glorified God and blessed you:

2ND QUARTER GOALS

Today's Plan

Day of the Week: Date:

To Do:

Schedule:

Dinner:

Notes:

Outfit:

Monthly Tasks- Month of:

Monthly Tasks- Month of:

Monthly Tasks- Month of:

Quarterly Recap

- What was the smartest thing you did this quarter?

- What 3 things happened you never want to happen again?

- What are 3 things that went really well?

- List 3 things you feel you could have done better:

- Pick 1 act of service you did that helped another person, glorified God and blessed you:

3RD QUARTER GOALS

Today's Plan

Day of the Week: Date:

To Do:

Schedule:

Dinner:

Notes:

Outfit:

Monthly Tasks- Month of:

Monthly Tasks- Month of:

Monthly Tasks- Month of:

Quarterly Recap

- What was the smartest thing you did this quarter?

- What 3 things happened you never want to happen again?

- What are 3 things that went really well?

- List 3 things you feel you could have done better:

- Pick 1 act of service you did that helped another person, glorified God and blessed you:

4THQUARTER GOALS

Today's Plan

Day of the Week: **Date:**

To Do:

Schedule:

Dinner:

Notes:

Outfit:

Monthly Tasks- Month of:

Monthly Tasks- Month of:

Monthly Tasks- Month of:

Quarterly Recap

- What was the smartest thing you did this quarter?

- What 3 things happened you never want to happen again?

- What are 3 things that went really well?

- List 3 things you feel you could have done better:

- Pick 1 act of service you did that helped another person that glorified God, blessed them and blessed you:

32552902R00097

Made in the USA
Middletown, DE
05 January 2019